Providing Integrity, Awareness, and Consciousness in Distributed Dynamic Systems

The ideas of this book originate from the mobile WAVE approach which allowed us, more than a half century ago, to implement citywide heterogeneous computer networks and solve distributed problems on them well before the internet. The invented paradigm evolved into Spatial Grasp Technology and resulted in a European patent and eight books. The volumes covered concrete applications in graph and network theory, defense and social systems, crisis management, simulation of global viruses, gestalt theory, collective robotics, space research, and related concepts. The obtained solutions often exhibited high system qualities like global integrity, distributed awareness, and even consciousness. This current book takes these important characteristics as primary research objectives, together with the theory of patterns covering them all. This book is oriented towards system scientists, application programmers, industry managers, defense and security commanders, and university students (especially those interested in advanced MSc and PhD projects on distributed system management), as well as philosophers, psychologists, and United Nations personnel.

Peter Simon Sapaty, Chief Research Scientist, Ukrainian Academy of Sciences, has worked with networked systems for more than five decades. Outside of Ukraine, he worked in the former Czechoslovakia (now Slovak Republic), Germany, the UK, Canada, and Japan as a group leader, Alexander von Humboldt researcher, and invited and visiting professor. He launched and chaired the SIG on Mobile Cooperative Technologies in the Distributed Interactive Simulation project in the US and invented a distributed control technology that resulted in a European patent and books with Wiley, Springer, Emerald, and Taylor & Francis. He has published more than 270 papers on distributed systems and has been included in the Marquis Who's Who in the World and Cambridge Outstanding Intellectuals of the 21st Century. Peter also works with several international scientific journals as an editorial board member.

Providing Integrity, Awareness, and Consciousness in Distributed Dynamic Systems

Peter Simon Sapaty

CRC Press
Taylor & Francis Group
Boca Raton London New York

CRC Press is an imprint of the
Taylor & Francis Group, an **informa** business

Designed cover image: © Shutterstock

First edition published 2024
by CRC Press
2385 NW Executive Center Drive, Suite 320, Boca Raton FL 33431

and by CRC Press
4 Park Square, Milton Park, Abingdon, Oxon, OX14 4RN

CRC Press is an imprint of Taylor & Francis Group, LLC

ISBN: 978-1-032-54517-2 (hbk)
ISBN: 978-1-032-54518-9 (pbk)
ISBN: 978-1-003-42526-7 (ebk)

DOI: 10.1201/9781003425267

Typeset in Caslon
by Apex CoVantage, LLC

To my wife Lilia, from classmate to more than a half century in marriage—a wonderful adviser, psychologist, doctor, family planner, and talented cook—for her inspiration and support of this and all previous books.

Contents

Preface

The ideas of this book originate from the WAVE approach which allowed us, more than a half century ago, to implement citywide heterogeneous computer networks and solve distributed problems on them in very flexible and mobile way, well before the internet. The invented paradigm evolved into Spatial Grasp Technology and resulted in a European patent and eight books published by John Wiley, Springer, Emerald, and Taylor & Francis. The volumes covered concrete applications in graph and network theory, defense and social systems, crises management, simulation of global viruses, gestalt theory, collective robotics, space research, and many others. The obtained solutions often exhibited high system qualities like global integrity, distributed awareness, and even a sort of consciousness. The current book chooses these important characteristics as primary research objectives, together with the theory of patterns covering them. By first reviewing and classifying numerous existing ideas and publications in these areas, it then shows possible solutions in them with the technology developed, which may influence the development of advanced intelligent systems with many important applications. The obtained results can also provide additional ground and practical examples for consciousness-related theories, on which common opinions have not been reached yet due to their enormous diversity and complexity.

After dealing with the symbiosis of physical and virtual worlds under a holistic spatial model as in previous books and other publications, we can extend such integrity into the mental and spiritual world touched on in the current book. This could help develop advanced models of world economic, cultural, political, security, and military organizations, using for their simulation the most advanced computer, communication, and information systems and networks. The proper modification of such models, which can cooperate and compete with each other, also using their repeated simulation, may lead to real strategies effectively supporting world peace and prosperity.

Peter Simon Sapaty
August 2023
Kiev, Ukraine

Acknowledgements

With special thanks to my good colleagues, friends, and their organizations for the lasting support and active discussions of the ideas of this book:

John Page, University of New South Wales, Australia
Steve Lambacher, Aoyama Gakuin University, Tokyo, Japan
Kohei Arai, Saga University, Saga Prefecture, Japan
Bob Nugent, Catholic University of America, Washington, DC
Thomas Ditzinger, Editor of Springer Books, Germany
Jim White, former Vice President at General Magic, now Hawaii, USA
Melian Lee, *International Relations and Diplomacy* journal, David Publishing Company, USA
Svitlana Tymchyk, Nataliia Karevina, and **Yevheniia Petruk**, Editorial team of *Mathematical Machines and Systems* journal, National Academy of Sciences of Ukraine

1

INTRODUCTION

1.1 Word Problems, Book Goals, and the Approach Used

The main goal of this book is to enrich large distributed systems with important applications, as well as their management and control technologies, with some higher-level organizational features that can improve their performance, especially in complex situations. The whole world is an extremely complex heterogeneous, distributed, and dynamic system, actually a spatial organism with both body and mentality. The main threats to its well-being and even existence are represented by the UN list [1] covering the following issues.

1.1.1 Climate Change

One of the major problems is linked to the global temperatures that are continuously rising. Studies show that by 2100 there is a 50% likelihood of facing global warming that is higher than 3.5 degrees Celsius and a 10% probability of witnessing warming higher than 4.7 degrees Celsius. This would result in more severe shifts in weather patterns, food and resource shortages, and more rapid spread of diseases.

1.1.2 Wars and Military Conflicts

Maintaining peace and security is crucial to preventing poverty and high numbers of refugees and asylum seekers. With an increasing number of territories becoming conflict zones, the number of poor and displaced women and children is on rise, causing the spread of diseases and a halt to economic progress. Preventative diplomacy and demilitarization are the two key tactics for avoiding conflicts.

DOI: 10.1201/9781003425267-1

1.1.3 Water Contamination

There is no life without water—apparently a simple truth but one that people seem to overlook. Poor management and irrational use forces communities to migrate in search of drinking water. Industries are polluting underground water, and this issue is growing massively. Due to pollution, poverty, and inadequate resource management, around 2.1 billion people lack access to safe drinking water.

1.1.4 Human Rights Violations

Human rights are universal, regardless of race, gender, ethnicity, religion, or any other status, but what if this only happens on paper? Indeed, the problems in today's society are linked with the constant violation of human rights—gender inequality, human trafficking, the lack of freedom of speech—all of these can be witnessed in the 21st century in every country, even in developed nations.

1.1.5 Global Health Issues

Since its founding, the UN has been actively concerned with advocating and maintaining good health around the globe. Today, COVID-19 remains the top concern internationally. People continue to experience complex, linked dangers to their health. Air pollution and climate change have a serious impact on our health. Hurricanes, floods, and droughts make disease transmission easier among large populations of people.

1.1.6 Poverty

Global poverty represents one of the most serious problems in modern society. The world's poorest people frequently experience hunger, have limited access to proper education, often go without light at night, and face serious health problems. It has been estimated that around 60% of the world's population lives on less than US$10 per day and around 10% on less than US$1.90 per day.

1.1.7 Children's Poor Access to Healthcare, Education, and Safety

Every child must benefit from the right to proper healthcare, access to education, and living in safety, and every society benefits from increasing children's life prospects. Despite this, millions of children worldwide face serious challenges linked with their birthplace, gender, or circumstances.

1.1.8 Access to Food and Hunger

By 2030, it is less likely that the world will achieve Sustainable Development Goal 2: Zero Hunger, according to international agencies and media. The situation in countries that have faced food insecurity and where populations suffer from hunger has worsened further as a result of the health and socioeconomic effects of the COVID-19 pandemic.

1.1.9 Migration

Massive migration movements impact all United Nations Member States, necessitating greater collaboration and responsibility-sharing. The Member States endorsed the New York Declaration for Refugees and Migrants wherein they acknowledged that there is a need for a comprehensive strategy for migration.

1.1.10 Weapons Accessibility

Multilateral disarmament and armament restriction are the aims that have been important to the United Nations' attempts to keep international peace since its inception. The United Nations has placed a high priority on decreasing and ultimately eliminating nuclear weapons, abolishing chemical weapons, and reinforcing the ban on biological weapons, all of which pose the greatest dangers to humanity.

Although the mentioned 10 global issues certainly help to establish what governments and ordinary people around the world should focus on, there are many other problems that everyone should be aware of, including the aging of the population and law and justice (see many more at [2]). To fight all the problems mentioned and improve overall prosperity, increase stability, and orient the world's evolution in the most progressive way, some higher and global levels of self-comprehension, self-analysis, and self-management should be introduced and developed.

Towards accomplishing this, we will be using quite different organizational philosophy, model, and technology providing highly integral solutions by dynamic coverage and matching of distributed environments by active self-spreading recursive code, rather than treating and managing systems and their solutions as parts exchanging messages. It will be explained, as well as shown in practical examples, how this paradigm can effectively support distributed integrity and awareness of large systems and even simulate a sort of global consciousness in many important areas, which may include economy, ecology, climate, psychology, international relations, space conquest, security and defense, and others. The current book may be considered a sequel to the previous books on distributed management of large systems with the developed spatial model [3–10].

1.2 Other Books in the Areas Considered

A brief review of other books in the related areas, which effectively stimulated preparation of the current book and how it may differ from them, is provided next.

> *Managing Distributed Dynamic Systems with Spatial Grasp Technology* [5] describes a novel ideology and technology for holistic management and control of distributed dynamic systems. The current book highlights further technology improvements and their ability to implement and model much higher organizational levels covering global integrity, awareness, and even consciousness, with important applications of the enriched systems in civil, security, and defense areas.
>
> *The Routledge Handbook of Consciousness* [11] describes the explosion of work on consciousness with the need of bringing together experts on fundamental and cutting-edge topics. The current book expresses and explains different consciousness

ideas in a clear and simple way (including its brain-embedded, wavelike, migrating, and even outside body variants) using recursive Spatial Grasp Language with efficient implementation in distributed systems.

Consciousness-Based Leadership and Management [12] examines the need for a consciousness-based view of leadership with sustaining competitive advantage. The current book shows the possibilities of consciousness-supported leadership in both a centralized and a distributed way using Spatial Grasp Language, including meaning-making, capability flow, and others. The offered model and technology can be practically used for solving very complex management problems.

Designing for Situation Awareness [13] describes the need for effective interfaces to manage diverse information and understanding of what is currently happening and what will be next. The current book offers a practical distributed technology allowing for high-level situational awareness in military and intelligence operations, emergency management, air traffic control, business management, space exploration, and others.

Integrity, Internal Control and Security in Information Systems [14] explores how information integrity contributes to the overall control and governance frameworks that enterprises need to deliver. The current book describes a practical model and technology that can provide high integrity of control and security for many industries with enterprise survival as the hottest issues. It also shows how to organize distributed systems capable of self-recovery under any circumstances.

Climate Crisis and Consciousness [15] is about the challenges of dealing with climate and ecological crises and the importance of the consciousness idea for this. The current book offers a practical model and technology suitable for collective climate awareness and consciousness, as well as for the organization of rapid actions to reduce climate crises and their consequences on a worldwide scale.

Consciousness and Robot Sentience [16] provides insights into artificial intelligence and machine consciousness, with artificial creation of consciousness by associative neural networks.

The new book shows how such ideas can be simulated by the developed spatial model and technology, including creation of distributed associative networks. It also provides examples of spatial consciousness for robotic collectives with practical applications.

Solving the Mind–Body Problem by the CODAM Neural Model of Consciousness [17] tries to bridge the gap between philosophers of mind and neuroscience community with the neural consciousness model. The current book shows how to use Spatial Grasp Language for expressing the mind-body problem. It also stimulates other ideas about consciousness, even fantastic ones, like its migration or even existence outside body, which may be very useful for practical systems.

Applying Practical Security in Your World [18] provides the knowledge needed to protect computers and networks from sophisticated attacks, with computer security posing daunting challenges. The current book shows practical examples for fighting computer viruses, including tracing and discovering their sources, by engaging Spatial Grasp Technology, itself based on super-virus principles and used in the past within intelligent network management projects.

Consciousness and the World [19] puts forward a bold theory of consciousness with philosophical elucidation of its nature, as well as concrete interaction between consciousness and the world. The current book also links these two concepts but in very practical way, where enriching management and control of business, security, and defense organizations with consciousness can improve overall performance and the world as a whole.

1.3 Summary of the Book Chapters

1.3.1 Chapter 2: Spatial Grasp Model and Technology Basics

Chapter 2 briefs the developed Spatial Grasp (SG) paradigm and resultant Spatial Grasp Technology (SGT), discussing the main paradigm idea by which distributed worlds, which may be physical, virtual, or executive in nature, are directly navigated by active self-spreading scenarios written in high-level Spatial Grasp Language (SGL) [3–10, 20–29]. The discussed SGL features include its deeply recursive structure and different types of used constants, variables, and universal rules providing any processing, management, control, and contextual capabilities. The chapter explains how SGL scenarios evolve in distributed spaces managed with special control states and describes distributed SGL implementation details, revealing the interpreter's internal organization, behavior of the interpretation network as a powerful spatial engine, and organization of its tracking system behaving as global control over the spreading spatial processes. The chapter also compares the described technology with works on mobile agents and related language Telescript [30, 31], acknowledging that SGT and SG, assigning the mobile feature to the whole programming ideology and methodology, represent a much more universal and powerful concept.

1.3.2 Chapter 3: Spatial Grasp Language Details

Chapter 3 provides key Spatial Grasp Language details (more in [3–10, 21–26, 29]), information on which may be particularly useful for proper understanding of numerous practical examples using SGL code in the subsequent chapters. It describes different types of SGL constants that can be self-identifiable by the way they are written or defined by special rules in general case, including information, physical matter, special constants, compound constants, and custom constants. The chapter presents different types of SGL variables with their semantics, spatial distribution, and movement, which include global variables, heritable variables, frontal variables, nodal variables, and environmental variables. The full repertoire of SGL rules are then provided with their semantics and practical use, which include type, usage, movement, creation, echoing, verification, assignment, advancement, branching, transference, exchange, timing, qualification, and grasping, finally summarizing the full SGL syntax.

1.3.3 Chapter 4: Distributed System Integrity under Spatial Grasp Technology

Chapter 4 investigates the applicability and efficiency of SGT for organizing and supporting the integrity of large distributed systems, which may cover any physical and virtual space, first reviewing and classifying the existing works on integrity, security, and recovery of distributed systems [32–43]. Then it shows how to use SGL for distributed system topology representation and creation, starting from all nodes in parallel or from a single node in the spanning tree mode, and how to copy the already existing or just created system topology, also in two modes. The chapter shows how to create in SGL fully self-healing distributed topologies, which can self-reconstruct after simultaneous failures of any nodes, if at least a single node still remains alive. This may provide a universal solution for the system's immortality, to be effectively used for numerous applications from IT to industry to security to defense.

1.3.4 *Chapter 5: Providing Global Awareness in Distributed Dynamic Systems*

Awareness, especially its global capabilities, is extremely important in our everyday life. Chapter 5 investigates the application of SGT for solving diverse problems in large distributed dynamic systems, which can guarantee from any inside or outside point sufficient awareness of their coverage, structures, and functionalities. It provides classified review of the existing awareness approaches [44–58], emphasizing the complexity of real systems and the necessity for new approaches leading to their high awareness. The chapter analyzes in detail a distributed system example with 100 different nodes interlinked by various relations with virtual and physical properties. Elementary awareness queries are considered, which include qualities and names of certain kinds of nodes and finding different paths in the whole network. The chapter finds peculiar structures in the system network, reflecting its diversity and complexity, and also provides higher-level knowledge about the distributed system as a whole or its particular parts, including semantic links between them and physical areas occupied.

1.3.5 *Chapter 6: Simulating Distributed Consciousness with Spatial Grasp Model*

Chapter 6 investigates the applicability and efficiency of SGT for expressing and simulating different ideas and features of the extremely important but often controversial and not sufficiently investigated phenomenon of consciousness. It reviews and classifies existing works and publications on consciousness [59–96], and then shows an example in SGL for managing a swarm of chasers fighting targets on different levels, from embedded distributed awareness to consciousness-related capabilities which may be independent and freely wandering, or even outside. The chapter discusses global awareness and even consciousness of the whole country, showing simple spatial examples in SGL relating to its components, like finding images in pattern matching mode, outlining coordinates of a specific region, and broadcasting executive orders via satellite network. Consciousness-related features are discussed based on obtained global feelings, judgments, and opinions, which may influence the state and further development of the whole system, showing both centralized and wandering consciousness solutions. A summary is provided on investigated potential applications of SGT and SGL for different consciousness ideas and categories.

1.3.6 *Chapter 7: Managing Distributed Systems with Spatial Grasp Patterns*

Pattern can represent everything in both digital and physical worlds. Chapter 7 investigates and analyzes the applicability of the SGT and especially SGL for representation and implementation of different types of patterns that can be used in simulation and management of a variety of distributed dynamic systems. It reviews and classifies existing works on patterns [97–124], shows how patterns can be expressed in SGL, including regular patterns and patterns of concrete objects, and exhibits pattern-based solutions for coordinating a transport column, finding distributed zone coordinates, and spatial tracking of mobile objects. The chapter offers network examples for distributed pattern recognition and matching and provides a summary of the investigated use of SGL for patterns processing, which can be treated as a real and universal pattern language, with SGT contributing to pattern theory in general. This summary covers descriptive patterns, creative patterns, patterns as spatial processes, pattern recognition, self-matching patterns, combined patterns, cooperating and conflicting patterns, psychological patterns, and recursive patterns.

1.3.7 *Chapter 8: Conclusions*

With an excursion back into history, Chapter 8 mentions that the main ideas of this book originated from the mobile WAVE approach that allowed us to implement citywide heterogeneous computer networks and solve distributed problems on them more than a half century ago, well before the internet. This approach evolved into the Spatial Grasp Model and Technology, which provided results in the current book's areas of system integrity, awareness, consciousness, and pattern recognition, with solution excerpts from different chapters exhibited. The investigated areas are then integrated into a holistic system to be used jointly in the design of distributed intelligent systems. The chapter mentions planned new research on spatial awareness, psychological patterns, and consciousness flexibility, as well as the importance of psychology and psychiatry for international relations, mentioning the related correspondence between Albert Einstein and Sigmund Freud. It concludes with the book's results in general, technology implementation issues, and market orientation. The references provided point at numerous ideas and publications used and classified within the researched areas.

References

1. D. Filipenco, Top 10 World Problems and Their Solutions, 2 August 2022. www.developmentaid.org/news-stream/post/147458/top-10-world-problems-and-their-solutions
2. 100+ Ways to Heal the Planet. https://healtheplanet.com/100-ways-to-heal-the-planet/?gad=1&gclid=CjwKCAjwwb6lBhBJEiwAbuVUShK 86HiW8uXefpY3xL4TuXJBh1JKb86k652trpLSUuOveyGoDyU 0zRoCAxUQAvD_BwE
3. P. S. Sapaty, Mobile Processing in Distributed and Open Environments. New York: John Wiley & Sons, 1999.
4. P. S. Sapaty, Ruling Distributed Dynamic Worlds. New York: John Wiley & Sons, 2005.
5. P. S. Sapaty, Managing Distributed Dynamic Systems with Spatial Grasp Technology. Springer, 2017.
6. P. S. Sapaty, Holistic Analysis and Management of Distributed Social Systems. Springer, 2018.
7. P. S. Sapaty, Complexity in International Security: A Holistic Spatial Approach. Emerald Publishing, 2019.
8. P. S. Sapaty, Symbiosis of Real and Simulated Worlds Under Spatial Grasp Technology. Springer, 2021.

9. P. S. Sapaty, Spatial Grasp as a Model for Space-Based Control and Management Systems. CRC Press, 2022.
10. P. S. Sapaty, The Spatial Grasp Model: Applications and Investigations of Distributed Dynamic Worlds. Emerald Publishing, 2023.
11. R. J. Gennaro (Ed), The Routledge Handbook of Consciousness (Routledge Handbooks in Philosophy). Routledge, 2018.
12. A. K. Maheshwari (Ed), Consciousness-Based Leadership and Management, Volume 2: Organizational and Cultural Approaches to Oneness and Flourishing (Palgrave Studies in Workplace Spirituality and Fulfillment). Palgrave Macmillan, 2023.
13. M. R. Endsley, Designing for Situation Awareness: An Approach to User-Centered Design. CRC Press, 2011.
14. M. Gertz, E. Guldentops, L. A. M. Strous (Eds.), Integrity, Internal Control and Security in Information Systems: Connecting Governance and Technology (IFIP Advances in Information and Communication Technology Book 83). Springer, 2013.
15. S. Gillespie, Climate Crisis and Consciousness: Re-Imagining Our World and Ourselves. Routledge, 2019.
16. P. O. Haikonen, Consciousness and Robot Sentience (2nd Edition, Series on Machine Consciousness Book 4). World Scientific, 2019.
17. J. G. Taylor, Solving the Mind-Body Problem by the CODAM Neural Model of Consciousness? (Springer Series in Cognitive and Neural Systems Book 9). Springer, 2013.
18. M. Ciampa, Awareness: Applying Practical Security in Your World. Course Technology, 2016.
19. B. O'Shaughnessy, Consciousness and the World. Oxford: Oxford University Press, 2000.
20. P. S. Sapaty, A Distributed Processing System, European Patent N 0389655, Publ. 10.11.93. European Patent Office.
21. P. S. Sapaty, Relation of Spatial Grasp Paradigm to Higher Psychological and Mental Concepts, Acta Scientific Computer Sciences, 2022, 4(12). https://actascientific.com/ASCS/pdf/ASCS-04-0359.pdf
22. P. S. Sapaty, Seeing and Managing Distributed Worlds with Spatial Grasp Paradigm, Acta Scientific Computer Sciences, 2022, 4(12). https://actascientific.com/ASCS/pdf/ASCS-04-0365.pdf
23. P. S. Sapaty, Comprehending Distributed Worlds with the Spatial Grasp Paradigm, Mathematical Machines and Systems, 2022, 1. www.immsp.kiev.ua/publications/articles/2022/2022_1/01_22_Sapaty.pdf
24. P. S. Sapaty, Spatial Management of Air and Missile Defence Operations, Mathematical Machines and Systems, 2023, 1. www.immsp.kiev.ua/publications/articles/2023/2023_1/01_23_Sapaty.pdf
25. P. S. Sapaty, Providing Distributed System Integrity Under Spatial Grasp Technology, Mathematical Machines and Systems, 2023, 2. www.immsp.kiev.ua/publications/articles/2023/2023_2/02_23_Sapaty.pdf
26. P. S. Sapaty, Providing Global Awareness in Distributed Dynamic Systems, International Relations and Diplomacy, 2023, 11(2), 87–100. https://doi.org/10.17265/2328-2134/2023.02.002. www.davidpublisher.com/Public/uploads/Contribute/6486c3d05a6cc.pdf

27. A. T. Bondarenko, S. B. Mikhalevich, A. I. Nikitin, P. S. Sapaty, Software of BESM-6 Computer for Communication with Peripheral Computers via Telephone Channels. In Computer Software, Vol. 5. Kiev: Institute of Cybernetics Press, 1970.

28. P. S. Sapaty, A Method of Organization of an Intercomputer Dialogue in the Radial Computer Systems. In The Design of Software and Hardware for Automatic Control Systems. Kiev: Institute of Cybernetics Press, 1973.

29. P. S. Sapaty, A Wave Language for Parallel Processing of Semantic Networks, Computing and Artificial Intelligence, 1986, 5(4), 289–314.

30. Mobile Agent. https://en.wikipedia.org/wiki/Mobile_agent

31. Telescript Language Reference, General Magic, October 1995. http://bitsavers.informatik.uni-stuttgart.de/pdf/generalMagic/Telescript_Language_Reference_Oct95.pdf

32. M. Mittal, R. Sangani, K. Srivastava, Testing Data Integrity in Distributed Systems, Procedia Computer Science, 2015, 45, 446–452. www.sciencedirect.com/science/article/pii/S1877050915003130

33. T. Rauter, Integrity of Distributed Control Systems. Student Forum of the 46th Annual IEEE/IFIP International Conference on Dependable Systems and Networks (hal-01318372), Toulouse, June 2016. https://hal.science/hal-01318372/file/DSN-Student-Forum_%237_Integrity-of-Distributed-Control-Systems.pdf

34. G. Sivanandham, J. M. Gnanasekar, Data Integrity and Recovery Management in Cloud Systems. Proceedings of the Fourth International Conference on Inventive Systems and Control (ICISC 2020) DVD Part Number: CFP20J06-DVD. www.researchgate.net/publication/343751352_Data_Integrity_and_Recovery_Management_in_Cloud_Systems

35. G. K. Sodhi, Recovery and Security in Distributed System, International Journal of Advanced Research in Computer and Communication Engineering, 2015, 4(12). www.ijarcce.com/upload/2015/december-15/IJARCCE%20105.pdf

36. X. Sun, J. Chen, H. Zhao, W. Zhang, Y. Zhang, Sequential Disaster Recovery Strategy for Resilient Distribution Network Based on Cyber–Physical Collaborative Optimization, IEEE Transactions on Smart Grid, 2023, 14(2), 1173–1187. https://doi.org/10.1109/TSG.2022.3198696. https://ieeexplore.ieee.org/document/9857641

37. V. Popa-Simil, H. Poston, Thomas, L. Popa-Simil, Self-Recovery of a Distributed System After a Large Disruption, New Mexico Supercomputing Challenge, Final Report, 1 April 2012. www.supercomputingchallenge.org/11-12/finalreports/15.pdf

38. Y. Watanabe, S. Sato, Y. Ishida, An Approach for Self-Repair in Distributed System Using Immunity-Based Diagnostic Mobile Agents. In Negoita, M. G. et al. (Eds.), KES 2004, LNAI 3214. Berlin and Heidelberg: Springer-Verlag, 2004, pp. 504–510. https://link.springer.com/chapter/10.1007/978-3-540-30133-2_66

39. A. M. Farley, A. Proskurowski, Minimum Self-Repairing Graphs, Graphs and Combinatorics, 1997, 13, 345–351. https://doi.org/10.1007/BF03353012. https://link.springer.com/article/10.1007/BF03353012

40. I. B. Hafaiedh, M. B. Slimane, A Distributed Formal-Based Model for Self-Healing Behaviors in Autonomous Systems: From Failure Detection to Self-Recovery, The Journal of Supercomputing, 2022, 78, 18725–18753. https://link.springer.com/article/10.1007/s11227-022-04614-0

41. J. Nikolic, N. Jubatyrov, E. Pournaras, Self-Healing Dilemmas in Distributed Systems: Fault Correction vs. Fault Tolerance, Journal of Latex Class Files, 2021, X(X). https://arxiv.org/pdf/2007.05261.pdf

42. W. Quattrociocchi, G. Caldarelli, A. Scala, Self-Healing Networks: Redundancy and Structure, PLoS One, 2014, 9(2), e87986. file:///C:/Users/user/Downloads/2014-02Self-healingnetworksredundancyand structure.pdf

43. A. Rodríguez, J. Gómez, A. Diaconescu, A Decentralised Self-Healing Approach for Network Topology Maintenance, Autonomous Agents and Multi-Agent Systems, 2021, 35, Article Number 6. https://link.springer.com/article/10.1007/s10458-020-09486-3

44. Awareness. https://en.wikipedia.org/wiki/Awareness

45. What Is Spatial Awareness? https://numeracyforallab.ca/what-we-learned/developing-spatial-awareness/

46. Total Information Awareness. https://en.wikipedia.org/wiki/Total_Information_Awareness

47. R. Mohanan, What Are Distributed Systems? Architecture Types, Key Components, and Examples, 12 January 2022. www.spiceworks.com/tech/cloud/articles/what-is-distributed-computing/

48. P. M. Salmon, K. L. Plant, Distributed Situation Awareness: From Awareness in Individuals and Teams to the Awareness of Technologies, Sociotechnical Systems, and Societies, Applied Ergonomics, 2022, 98, 103599. www.sciencedirect.com/science/article/abs/pii/S0003687021002465

49. N. A. Stanton, Distributed Situation Awareness, Contemporary Ergonomics and Human Factors. In Charles, R., Wilkinson, J. (Eds.), CIEHF, 2016. https://publications.ergonomics.org.uk/uploads/Distributed-Situation-Awareness.pdf

50. M. M. Chatzimichailidou, A. Protopapas, I. M. Dokas, Seven Issues on Distributed Situation Awareness Measurement in Complex Socio-Technical Systems. In Boulanger, F., Krob, D., Morel, G., Roussel, J. C. (Eds.), Complex Systems Design & Management. Cham: Springer, 2015. https://doi.org/10.1007/978-3-319-11617-4_8. https://link.springer.com/chapter/10.1007/978-3-319-11617-4_8

51. E. Sultanov, E. Weber, Real World Awareness in Distributed Organizations: A View on Informal Processes, 2011. www.researchgate.net/publication/234720130_Real_World_Awareness_in_Distributed_Organizations_A_View_on_Informal_Processes

52. P. M. Salmon, N. A. Stanton, D. P. Jenkins, Distributed Situation Awareness Theory, Measurement and Application to Teamwork, By Copyright 2009, Published 31 March 2017 by CRC Press. www.routledge.com/Distributed-Situation-Awareness-Theory-Measurement-and-Application-to/Salmon-Stanton-Jenkins/p/book/9781138073852

53. M. M. Chatzimichailidou, R. Freund, I. Dokas, Distributed Situation Awareness as a "Middleware" Between the New Economic Sociology and Embedded Open Innovation. 6th International Conference on Mass Customization and Personalization in Central Europe (MCP-CE 2014). https://mcp-ce.org/wp-content/uploads/proceedings/2014/6_chatzimi-chailidou.pdf

54. J. S. Preden, J. Helander, Context Awareness in Distributed Computing Systems, Annales Univ. Sci. Budapest., Sect. Comp., 2009, 31, 57–73. www.researchgate.net/publication/255564252_Context_Awareness_in_Distributed_Computing_Systems

55. S. Jones, E. Milner, M. Sooriyabandara, S. Hauert, Distributed Situational Awareness in Robot Swarms, Advanced Intelligent Systems, 2020, 2. https://onlinelibrary.wiley.com/doi/10.1002/aisy.202000110

56. S. K. Gan, Z. Xu, S. Sukkarieh, Distributed Situational Awareness and Control, UAS Multi-Vehicle Cooperation and Coordination, 13 June 2016. https://onlinelibrary.wiley.com/doi/full/10.1002/9780470686652.eae1133

57. L. Ge, Y. Li, J. Yan, Y. Sun, Smart Distribution Network Situation Awareness for High-Quality Operation and Maintenance: A Brief Review, Energies, 2022, 15(3), 828. https://doi.org/10.3390/en15030828

58. J. Tanveer, A. Haider, R. Ali, A. Kim, An Overview of Reinforcement Learning Algorithms for Handover Management in 5G Ultra-Dense Small Cell Networks, Applied Sciences, 2022, 12(1), 426. https://doi.org/10.3390/app12010426. www.mdpi.com/2076-3417/12/1/426

59. Consciousness. https://en.wikipedia.org/wiki/Consciousness

60. Hard Problem of Consciousness. https://en.wikipedia.org/wiki/Hard_problem_of_consciousness

61. M. Graziano, A New Theory Explains How Consciousness Evolved, The Atlantic, 6 June 2016. www.theatlantic.com/science/archive/2016/06/how-consciousness-evolved/485558/

62. K. Schultz, Consciousness: Definition, Examples, & Theory. The Berkeley Well-Being Institute, 2023. www.berkeleywellbeing.com/consciousness.html

63. A. Pereira Jr., The Projective Theory of Consciousness: From Neuroscience to Philosophical Psychology, Trans/Form/Ação, Marília, 2018, 41, 199–232. www.scielo.br/j/trans/a/5xcwgRK9wtfkf4Wm48FKGfv/?format=pdf&lang=en

64. Models of Consciousness. https://en.wikipedia.org/wiki/Models_of_consciousness

65. A. Seth, Models of Consciousness, Scholarpedia, 2007, 2(1), 1328. www.scholarpedia.org/article/Models_of_consciousness

66. D. Rudrauf, D. Bennequin, I. Granic, G. Landini, K. Friston, K. Williford, A Mathematical Model of Embodied Consciousness, Journal of Theoretical Biology, 2017, 428, 106–131. www.sciencedirect.com/science/article/abs/pii/S0022519317302540

67. Artificial Consciousness. https://en.wikipedia.org/wiki/Artificial_consciousness

68. P. O. Haikonen, Consciousness and Robot Sentience (2nd Edition, Machine Consciousness). World Scientific, 2019. www.amazon.com/Consciousness-Robot-Sentience-2nd-Machine/dp/9811205043

69. A. Sloman, R. Chrisley, Virtual Machines and Consciousness, Journal of Consciousness Studies, 2003, 10(4–5). www.cs.bham.ac.uk/research/projects/cogaff/sloman-chrisley-jcs03.pdf

70. P. Krauss, A. Maier, Will We Ever Have Conscious Machines? Frontiers in Computational Neuroscience, 2020, 14. https://doi.org/10.3389/fncom.2020.556544. www.frontiersin.org/articles/10.3389/fncom.2020.556544/full

71. P. Sjöstedt-H, Consciousness and Higher Spatial Dimensions, 14 April 2022. https://iai.tv/articles/consciousness-and-higher-spatial-dimensions-auid-2107

72. T. Das, Brain Waves Create Consciousness, International Journal of Development Research, 2018, 8(6), 20910–20912. www.journalijdr.com/brain-waves-create-consciousness

73. R. Pepperell, Consciousness as a Physical Process Caused by the Organization of Energy in the Brain, Consciousness Research, 2018, 9. www.frontiersin.org/articles/10.3389/fpsyg.2018.02091/full

74. B. Bower, Spreading Consciousness, Awareness Goes Global in the Brain, Science News, 15 October 2002. www.sciencenews.org/article/spreading-consciousness

75. C. N. Lazarus, Can Consciousness Exist Outside of the Brain? The Brain May Not Create Consciousness But "Filter" It, Psychology Today, 26 June 2019. www.psychologytoday.com/intl/blog/think-well/201906/can-consciousness-exist-outside-the-brain

76. H. Wahbeh, D. Radin, C. Cannard, A. Delorme, What If Consciousness Is Not an Emergent Property of the Brain? Observational and Empirical Challenges to Materialistic Models, Frontiers in Psychology, 2022, 13. www.frontiersin.org/articles/10.3389/fpsyg.2022.955594/full

77. R. Manzotti, The Spread Mind: Why Consciousness and the World Are One. OR Books, 2018. www.amazon.com/Spread-Mind-Why-Consciousness-World/dp/1944869492

78. J. Smallwood, J. W. Schooler, The Science of Mind Wandering: Empirically Navigating the Stream of Consciousness, Annual Review of Psychology, 2015, 66, 487–518. https://pubmed.ncbi.nlm.nih.gov/25293689/

79. M. Pearce, Gestalt: Beyond the Conscious Mind, 2 May 2019. https://touchedbyahorse.com/gestalt-beyond-the-conscious-mind/

80. R. V. De Walker, Consciousness Is Pattern Recognition. Computer Science > Artificial Intelligence [Submitted on 4 May 2016 (v1), last revised 28 Jun 2016 (this version, v2)]. https://arxiv.org/abs/1605.03009

81. G. Eoyang, Patterns for Consciousness, November 2014. www.hsdinstitute. org/resources/patterns-for-consciousness-blog.html

82. Patterns of the Consciousness – An Introduction. www.renxueinternational. org/patterns-of-the-consciousness-an-introduction/

83. S. Pockett, Consciousness Is a Thing, Not a Process, Applied Sciences, 2017, 7(12), 1248. www.mdpi.com/2076-3417/7/12/1248

84. T. A. Carey, Consciousness as Control and Controlled Perception, Annals of Behavioral Science, 2018, 4(2), 3. https://behaviouralscience. imedpub.com/consciousness-as-control-and-controlled-perception-a-perspective.php?aid=23059

85. J. Shepherd, Conscious Control Over Action, Mind & Language, 2015, 30(3), 320–344. https://doi.org/10.1111/mila.12082. https://onlinelibrary. wiley.com/doi/full/10.1111/mila.12082

86. D. F. Marks, I Am Conscious, Therefore, I Am: Imagery, Affect, Action, and a General Theory of Behavior, Brain Sciences, 2019, 9(5), 107. https:// doi.org/10.3390/brainsci9050107. www.mdpi.com/2076-3425/9/5/107

87. K. R. Balapala, Conscious and Subconscious Processes of Human Mind. A Clandestine Entity Indeed! International Journal of Basic and Applied Medical Sciences, 2014, 4(1). www.cibtech.org/J-MEDICAL-SCIENCES/PUBLICATIONS/2014/Vol_4_No_1/JMS-63-077-KARTHEEK-CONSCIOUS-INDEED.pdf

88. Collective Consciousness. https://en.wikipedia.org/wiki/Collective_consciousness

89. P. S. Sapaty, Simulating Distributed and Global Consciousness Under Spatial Grasp Paradigm, Advances in Machine Learning & Artificial Intelligence, 2020, 1(1). www.opastpublishers.com/open-access-articles/simulating-distributed-and-global-consciousness-under-spatial-grasp-paradigm.pdf

90. P. S. Sapaty, Simulating Distributed and Global Consciousness Under Spatial Grasp Paradigm, Mathematical Machines and Systems, 2020, 4. www.immsp.kiev.ua/publications/articles/2020/2020_4/Sapaty_04_20.pdf

91. P. Sapaty, Symbiosis of Real and Simulated Worlds Under Global Awareness and Consciousness. Abstract at: The Science of Consciousness Conference, TSC, 14–18 September 2020. https://eagle.sbs.arizona.edu/sc/report_poster_detail.php?abs=3696

92. K. Cherry, Consciousness in Psychology, 19 May 2023. www.verywellmind. com/what-is-consciousness-2795922

93. J. Sutton, Consciousness in Psychology: 8 Theories & Examples, 3 January 2021. https://positivepsychology.com/consciousness-psychology/

94. N. A. Conti, E. Keegan, F. Torrente, J. C. Stagnaro, Consciousness in Psychiatry, Vertex, 2008, 19(78), 19–28. www.researchgate.net/publication/5261624_Consciousness_in_psychiatry

95. Consciousness and Its Disorders. www.wikilectures.eu/w/Consciousness_and_its_disorders

96. J. M. Mecklin, The International Conscience, International Journal of Ethics, 1919, 29(3). www.jstor.org/stable/pdf/2377426.pdf
97. Pattern. https://en.wikipedia.org/wiki/Pattern
98. U. Grenander, M. Miller, Pattern Theory: From Representation to Inference (Oxford Studies in Modern European Culture). Oxford University Press, 2007. www.amazon.com/Pattern-Theory-Representation-Inference-European/dp/0199297061
99. D. Mumford, Pattern Theory: A Unifying Perspective, Supported by NSF Grant DMS 91-21266 and by the Geometry Center, University of Minnesota, 28 September 1992. www.dam.brown.edu/people/mumford/vision/papers/1994c-96--PattThUnifyingPersp-NC.pdf
100. F. D. M. de Souza, S. Sarkar, A. Srivastava, J. Su, Pattern Theory-Based Interpretation of Activities. 22nd International Conference on Pattern Recognition, 2014. https://projet.liris.cnrs.fr/imagine/pub/proceedings/ICPR-2014/data/5209a106.pdf
101. Pattern Theory. https://en.wikipedia.org/wiki/Pattern_theory
102. U. Joshi, Patterns of Distributed Systems, 7 September 2022. https://martinfowler.com/articles/patterns-of-distributed-systems/
103. T. Sankey, Statistical Descriptions of Spatial Patterns. In Shekhar, S., Xiong, H., Zhou, X. (Eds.), Encyclopedia of GIS. Cham: Springer, 2017. https://doi.org/10.1007/978-3-319-17885-1_1351. https://link.springer.com/referenceworkentry/10.1007/978-3-319-17885-1_1351
104. D. A. Keim, P. Kröger, M. Ankerst, Recursive Pattern: A Technique for Visualizing Very Large Amounts of Data. IEEE Xplore, Conference: Visualization, 1995. https://doi.org/10.1109/VISUAL.1995.485140. www.researchgate.net/publication/3618236_Recursive_pattern_A_technique_for_visualizing_very_large_amounts_of_data
105. B. Goertzel, The Hidden Pattern: A Patternist Philosophy of Mind, the Kurzweil Library + Collections, 27 December 2014. www.kurzweilai.net/the-hidden-pattern-a-patternist-philosophy-of-mind-2
106. N. Russell, A. H. M. ter Hofstede, W. M. P. van der Aalst, N. Mulyar, Workflow Control-Flow Patterns: A Revised View, 2006. www.workflowpatterns.com/documentation/documents/BPM-06-22.pdf
107. W. M. P. van der Aalst, A. H. M. der Hofstede, B. Kiepuszewski, A.P. Barros, Workflow Patterns, 2002. www.workflowpatterns.com/documentation/documents/wfs-pat-2002.pdf
108. Pattern Matching. https://en.wikipedia.org/wiki/Pattern_matching
109. J. Cheng, J. Xu Yu, B. Ding, P. S. Yu, H. Wang, Fast Graph Pattern Matching. www.microsoft.com/en-us/research/wp-content/uploads/2016/02/icde08gsearch.pdf
110. T. Reza, Pattern Matching in Massive Metadata Graphs at Scale, 2019. https://doi.org/10.14288/1.0387453. https://open.library.ubc.ca/soa/cIRcle/collections/ubctheses/24/items/1.0387453
111. Pattern Recognition. https://en.wikipedia.org/wiki/Pattern_recognition
112. R. Van De Walker, Consciousness Is Pattern Recognition, 2016. https://arxiv.org/abs/1605.03009

113. Pattern Recognition (Psychology). https://en.wikipedia.org/wiki/Pattern_recognition_(psychology)
114. Pattern Language. https://en.wikipedia.org/wiki/Pattern_language
115. Pattern Language. https://en.wikipedia.org/wiki/Pattern_language#:~:text=A%20pattern%20language%20is%20an,1977%20book%20A%20Pattern%20Language
116. A Pattern Language. https://en.wikipedia.org/wiki/A_Pattern_Language
117. What Is a Pattern Language? https://groupworksdeck.org/pattern-language
118. C. Alexander, S. Ishikawa, M. Silverstein, et al., A Pattern Language: Towns, Buildings, Construction (Center for Environmental Structure Series). Oxford University Press, 1977. www.amazon.com/Pattern-Language-Buildings-Construction-Environmental/dp/0195019199
119. T. Winn, P. Calder, A Pattern Language for Pattern Language Structure. Appeared at Third Asian Pacific Conference on Pattern Languages of Programs (KoalaPLoP 2002), January 2003. www.researchgate.net/publication/228944468_A_pattern_language_for_pattern_language_structure
120. M. Hafiz, P. Adamczyk, R. Johnson, Growing a Pattern Language (for Security), Proceedings of the ACM International Symposium on New Ideas, New Paradigms, and Reflections on Programming and Software, October 2012. https://doi.org/10.1145/2384592.2384607. www.researchgate.net/publication/262211609_Growing_a_pattern_language_for_security
121. T. Iba, Pattern Languages as Media for the Creative Society, Journal of Information Processing and Management, 2013, 55(12). https://doi.org/10.1241/johokanri.55.865. www.researchgate.net/publication/255484746_Pattern_Languages_as_Media_for_the_Creative_Society
122. T. Iba, Change Making Patterns. A Pattern Language for Fostering Social Entrepreneurship. https://citeseerx.ist.psu.edu/viewdoc/download?doi=10.1.1.677.5339&rep=rep1&type=pdf
123. M. Van Welie, G. van der Veer, Pattern Languages in Interaction Design: Structure and Organization, October 2011. www.researchgate.net/publication/228881522_Pattern_languages_in_interaction_design_Structure_and_organization
124. G. Meszaros, J. Doble, A Pattern Language for Pattern Writing, The Hillside Group. https://hillside.net/index.php/a-pattern-language-for-pattern-writing

2

Spatial Grasp Model and Technology Basics

2.1 Introduction

The chapter briefs the developed Spatial Grasp (SG) paradigm and resultant Spatial Grasp Technology (SGT) and is organized as follows. Section 2.2 discusses the main technology idea by which distributed worlds, which may be physical, virtual, or executive in nature, and any of their combinations, are directly navigated by active self-spreading scenarios written in high-level Spatial Grasp Language (SGL). Section 2.3 highlights the features of SGL, including its deeply recursive structure and different types of used constants, variables, and rules, providing any processing, management, control, and contextual capabilities, and summarizing the language in both textual and graphical form. The section explains how SGL scenarios evolve in distributed environments and how they are managed with special control states. Section 2.4 describes distributed SGL implementation capabilities, revealing the interpreter's internal organization, behavior of the interpretation network as a powerful spatial engine, and the organization of its tracking system behaving as the global control over spreading and echoing spatial processes. Section 2.5 compares the described technology with the idea of mobile agents and related language Telescript, acknowledging that despite also being based on code mobility, SGT and SGL assign this global feature to the whole programming ideology, allowing it to keep unlimited functionality and power within parallel self-spreading and self-matching code in distributed networks. Section 2.6 concludes the chapter.

2.2 Main Technology Ideas

Within the Spatial Grasp model and resulting Technology (SGT), a high-level scenario for any task to be performed in a distributed world

DOI: 10.1201/9781003425267-2   **19**

is represented as an active self-evolving pattern rather than a traditional sequential or parallel program (as by patent [1], books [2–9], and more [10–66]). This pattern, written in a high-level Spatial Grasp Language and expressing top semantics of the problem to be solved, can start from any point in the world. Then it spatially propagates, replicates, modifies, covers, and matches the distributed world in a parallel wavelike mode, while echoing the reached control states and data found or obtained for making decisions at higher levels and further space navigation, as symbolically shown in Figure 2.1.

This concept is based on a quite different philosophy of dealing with large distributed systems. Instead of representing systems and solutions in them in the form of communicating parts or agents, the developed Spatial Grasp paradigm organizes everything by the integral, holistic, and parallel substance covering and conquering distributed worlds, which may be as follows:

Physical World (PW), considered as continuous and infinite where each point can be identified and accessed by physical coordinates.

Virtual World (VW), which is discrete and consists of nodes and semantic links between them.

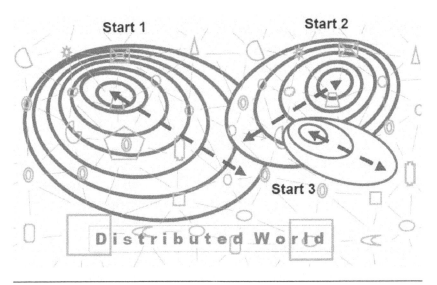

Figure 2.1 Spatial grasp model main idea.

Executive World (EW), consisting of active "doers," which may be humans or robots, with communication possibilities between them.

Different kinds of combinations of these worlds can also be possible within the same formalism, like Virtual-Physical World (VPW), Virtual-Executive World (VEW), Executive-Physical World (EPW), and Virtual-Executive-Physical World (VEPW), which combines all of the previous features.

2.3 Spatial Grasp Language Features

- **Language recursive structure**

The language top-level recursive organization can be expressed just by a single string, in a formula-like mode, as follows:

grasp → *constant* | *variable* | *rule* ({*grasp*,})

An SGL scenario, called *grasp*, applied in some point of the distributed space, can just be a *constant* directly providing the result to be associated with this point. It can be a *variable* whose content, assigned to it previously when staying in this or another space point (as variables may have non-local meaning and coverage), provides the result in the application point too. It can also be a *rule* (expressing certain ordering, action, control, description, or context) optionally accompanied with operands separated by comma and embraced in parentheses. These operands can be of any nature and complexity (including arbitrary scenarios themselves) and defined recursively as *grasp* again, that is, they can be *constants*, *variables*, or any *rules* with operands.

Some information on constants, variables, and rules follows.

- **SGL constants**

Constants are self-identifiable by the way they are written. They can also be explicitly defined by special embracing rules for arbitrary textual representations. They may be:

Information—as arbitrary strings in single quotes (which may be nested, if multiple), also numbers in traditional representations.

Physical matter or physical objects—as any texts in double quotes (which can be nested too) identifying adequately these elements.

Special or reserved constants—which may be used as standard parameters or modifiers in different language rules.

Custom items—special self-identifiable names/words established additionally by customers to serve specific classes of problems (to be adjusted with SGL implementations).

Special items—constants can also represent special items, introduced for certain application areas.

Details on different constant types and their usage are provided in the next chapter.

- **SGL variables**

Their repertoire is as follows, all being self-identifiable or declared by special rules for any names:

Global variables (most expensive and rarely used), which can serve any SGL scenarios and be shared by them.

Heritable variables appearing within a scenario step and serving all subsequent steps.

Frontal variables serving and accompanying the scenario evolution, being transferred between subsequent steps.

Nodal variables as a property of the world positions reached by scenarios and shared with other scenarios in the same positions.

Environmental variables allowing us to access, analyze, and change different parameters of physical, virtual, and executive worlds during their navigation, also certain language interpretation features (as of the internal world).

Details on different variable types and their usage are provided in the next chapter.

- **SGL rules**

SGL rules, starting in world points, can organize navigation of the world sequentially, in parallel, or in any combination thereof, with their types listed as *type, usage, seeing, movement, creation, echoing, verification, assignment, advancement, branching, transference, exchange, timing, qualifying,* and *extension*.

The rules can result in staying in the same application point or cause movement to other world points with the obtained results to be left there. The points reached can become starting points for other rules. The rules, due to recursive language organization, can form arbitrary operational and control infrastructures expressing any sequential, parallel, hierarchical, centralized, localized, and mixed and up to fully decentralized and distributed algorithms. The concept of rule is dominant in SGL not only for diverse activities on data, knowledge, and physical matter, but also for overall management and control of any SGL scenarios. The next chapter provides full details on SGL rules, including their semantics and usage.

- **SGL top-level summary**

As already discussed, SGL's top-level structure can be summarized as follows, where both *constant* and *rule* can also be represented as compound elements, defined recursively as *grasp* again:

grasp	→	**constant	variable	rule ({***grasp***,})**
constant	→	**information	matter	custom	special	** *grasp*
variable	→	**global	heritable	frontal	nodal	**
		environmental
rule	→	**type	usage	seeing	movement	creation |**
		**echoing	verification	assignment	advance-**
		**ment	branching	transference	exchange	**
		**timing	qualifying	** *grasp*

SGL top-level organization with its recursive syntax can also be expressed graphically, as in Figure 2.2.

- **How SGL scenarios evolve**

Following are some hints on how SGL scenarios self-evolve in distributed environments.

a. SGL scenario is developing in *steps*, potentially parallel, with new steps produced on the results of previous steps.
b. Any step is always associated with a certain *point* or points of the world (physical, virtual, executive, or combined) from which the scenario is currently developing.
c. Each step provides a resultant *value* (single or multiple) representing information, matter, or both, and a resultant control *state*.

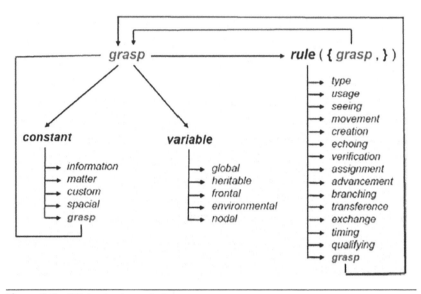

Figure 2.2 SGL top-level organization.

d. Different scenario parts may evolve from the same points in *ordered*, *unordered*, or *parallel* manner, as independent or interdependent branches.

e. Different scenario parts can spatially *succeed* each other, with new parts evolving from final positions reached by the previous parts.

f. This potentially parallel and distributed scenario may proceed in *synchronous* or *asynchronous* modes, as well as in any combination of them.

g. SGL operations and decisions can use *control states* and *values* returned from other, subsequent, scenario parts, combining forward and backward scenario evolution.

h. Different steps from the same or different scenarios may be temporarily associated with *same world points*, sharing persistent or provisional information in them.

i. Staying with different world points, whether physical or virtual, it may be possible to *change local parameters* in them, thus impacting the worlds via these locations.

j. Scenarios navigating distributed spaces can create active *distributed physical or virtual infrastructures* in them operating on their own, also shared with other scenarios.

k. Overall organization of the world creation, coverage, modification, analysis, and processing can be provided by a variety of SGL rules which may be *arbitrarily nested*.

l. The evolving SGL scenarios can *lose utilized parts* if not needed any more. They can also *self-modify* and *self-replicate* during space navigation, automatically adjusting to the distributed environments.

- **SGL control states**

The following control states appear after completion of different scenario steps, indicating their progress or failure. They can be used for effective control of multiple distributed processes with proper decisions at different levels.

thru—reflects full success of the current branch with capability of further scenario development.

done—indicates success of the current scenario step with its planned termination.

fail—indicates non-revocable failure of the current branch and no possibility of further development from the location reached.

fatal—reporting terminal failure in the location reached while triggering massive abortion of the currently evolving scenario processes, in other branches too, with deletion of associated temporary data in them. The level of such removal process can be controlled by special higher-level rules.

Full details of SGL are provided in Chapter 3.

2.4 Distributed SGL Implementation

- **Interpreter organization and structure**

The interpreter consists of a number of specialized functional modules, as in Figure 2.3 and later, working with specific data structures, both serving SGL scenarios or their parts that happen to be inside this interpreter at this moment of time, and also organizing exchanges with other interpreters in case of distributed SGL scenarios.

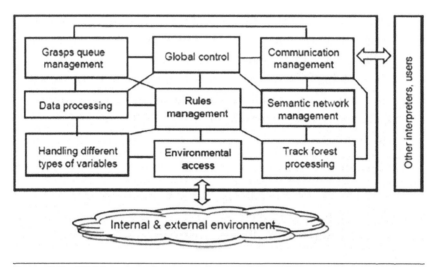

Figure 2.3 SGL interpreter main components and their interactions.

Grasps queue management—serving multiple SGL scenarios currently staying partially or entirely within the current interpreter copy, taking into account their priorities of just serving in a FIFO manner.

Data processing—executes different logical, numerical, and string operations activated by SGL rules, which may also include operations on physical matter and those providing access to external environment.

Handling different types of variables—keeps global, nodal, heritable, and environmental variables currently associated with the covered parts of virtual and physical spaces, also temporarily serves frontal variables before forwarding them to other interpreters.

Rules management—holds and implements semantics of different rules.

Semantic network management—keeps and processes part of the semantic network currently covered by the current interpreter, while supporting and processing links with its parts in other interpreters.

Track forest processing—organizes creation, support, and modification of distributed control tracks during spatial development of parallel scenarios, integrates with track forests in other interpreters, and also supports spatial variables (some being mobile) and forward-backward control propagation via the tracks.

Communication management—organizes and supports communications with other interpreters and users within integral spatial SGL solutions.

Environmental access—organizes and implements communications with external and internal virtual and physical environments based on the environmental variables.

Global control—supports integrity of multiple data processing, communications, and management solutions within the current interpreter (including timing of critical operations), also coordinating with global control in other interpreters to provide integrity of spatial solutions, which may have any terrestrial and celestial nature.

- **Interpreter network as a spatial engine**

Communicating interpreters of SGL can be in an arbitrary number of copies, up to millions and billions, which can be effectively integrated with any existing systems and communications, and their dynamic networks can represent *powerful spatial engines capable of solving any problems in terrestrial and celestial environments.* Such collective engines can simultaneously execute different cooperative or competitive scenarios without any central resources or control. Hardware or software SGL interpreters, shown in Figure 2.4 as

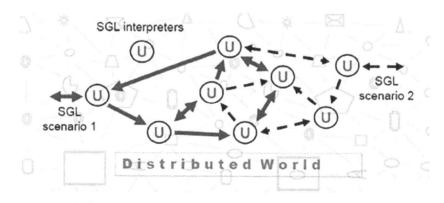

Figure 2.4 SGL distributed interpretation.

universal computational, control, and management units U, may be stationary or mobile. They can be dynamically installed, and if needed created, in proper physical or virtual world points on the request of self-evolving SGL scenarios.

- **Spatial tracking system**

As *both backbone and nerve system of the distributed interpreter,* its self-optimizing *spatial track system* provides hierarchical command and control, as well as remote data and code access. It also supports spatial variables and merges distributed control states for decisions at higher organizational levels. The track infrastructure is automatically distributed between active components (humans, robots, computers, smartphones, satellites, etc.) during scenario self-spreading in distributed environments. It integrates the following stages of operation (some stages of track system operation symbolically shown in Figure 2.5).

More details on the track operations follow.

2.4.1 Forward Grasping

In the forward process, the next steps of scenario development form new track nodes connected to the previous nodes by track links. Reflecting the history of scenario evolution, this growing track structure is effectively supporting heritable, nodal, and frontal variables associated with track nodes.

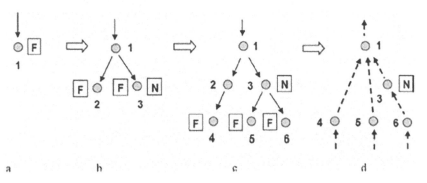

Figure 2.5   Different spatial track system operations. (a) Start with a single track node and frontal variable; (b) Track grows with replication of frontal variable and fixed support of nodal variable; (c) Further track growing with movement and replication of frontal variables; (d) Echoing via tracks with optimization of tracks structure and continuing support of the nodal variable.

2.4.2 Echoing

After completing the forward stage of SGL scenario, the track system can return to the starting track node the generalized control state based on termination states in all fringe nodes, also marking the passed track links with the states returned via them. The track system, on the request of higher-level scenario rules, can also collect the local data obtained at its fringe nodes and process them hierarchically and in parallel, or just merge them into a resultant list of values, to be echoed to the higher levels. The track echoing process also optimizes the track system by removing item that are already used and no longer needed.

2.4.3 Further Forward Development

The echo-modified and -optimized track system can route further grasps to the world positions reached by the previous grasps—to all or only part of them, as regards the higher-level decisions. Heritable variables created in certain track nodes can be also accessed from the subsequent nodes in the track system for both reading and writing operations.

2.5 Comparison with Mobile Agents and Telescript

A mobile agent [67] is a piece of software, combined with data, capable of migrating from one computer to another autonomously and continuing its execution at the destination. It is a process that can transport its state from one environment to another and can perform in the new environment. In the early 1990s, the US company General Magic created the Telescript language [68] and environment for writing and executing mobile agents. The earlier described Spatial Grasp Model and Technology is also based on code mobility in computer networks, but it assigns this global feature to the whole programming system in which self-replicating parts of spatial scenarios can propagate in parallel in distributed environments and communicate under recursive spatial control, also mobile. SGT keeps all functionality and power within self-replicating virus-like code with unlimited power to create, modify, control, and manage any distributed systems, actually existing independently of them. This paradigm (originally called WAVE) appeared much earlier than mobile agents and Telescript (from the end of the 1960s), and was practically used to organize distributed computations in citywide heterogeneous computer networks in Kiev, Ukraine, well before the internet [69–72]. The author visited James White, then vice president at General Magic and co-designer of Telescript in Seattle with a presentation of WAVE technology (also installed and operating at that time at the University of British Columbia in Vancouver, Canada).

2.6 Conclusions

General ideas of the mobile Spatial Grasp Technology and its basic Spatial Grasp Language have been summarized. The structure of SGL interpreter was briefed, with its communicating copies forming powerful parallel networked engines covering arbitrary large environments. The purpose and organization of the spatial tracking system of the interpreter effectively supporting spatial forward-backward capabilities of SGL have been explained. A comparison of SGT with mobile agents and the language Telescript have also been provided.

References

1. P. S. Sapaty, A Distributed Processing System, European Patent N 0389655, Publ. 10.11.93. European Patent Office.
2. P. S. Sapaty, Mobile Processing in Distributed and Open Environments. New York: John Wiley & Sons, 1999.
3. P. S. Sapaty, Ruling Distributed Dynamic Worlds. New York: John Wiley & Sons, 2005.
4. P. S. Sapaty, Managing Distributed Dynamic Systems with Spatial Grasp Technology. Springer, 2017.
5. P. S. Sapaty, Holistic Analysis and Management of Distributed Social Systems. Springer, 2018.
6. P. S. Sapaty, Complexity in International Security: A Holistic Spatial Approach. Emerald Publishing, 2019.
7. P. S. Sapaty, Symbiosis of Real and Simulated Worlds under Spatial Grasp Technology. Springer, 2021.
8. P. S. Sapaty, Spatial Grasp as a Model for Space-based Control and Management Systems. CRC Press, 2022.
9. P. S. Sapaty, The Spatial Grasp Model: Applications and Investigations of Distributed Dynamic Worlds. Emerald Publishing, 2023.

10. P. S. Sapaty, Distributed Artificial Brain for Collectively Behaving Mobile Robots. Proceedings of Symposium and Exhibition Unmanned Systems, Baltimore, MD, 31 July–2 August 2001.
11. P. S. Sapaty, Crisis Management with Distributed Processing Technology, International Transactions on Systems Science and Applications, 2006, 1(1), 81–92.
12. P. S. Sapaty, Global Management of Distributed EW-Related System. Proceedings of International Conference Electronic Warfare: Operations & Systems, Thistle, 2007.
13. P. S. Sapaty, Distributed Technology for Global Dominance. Proceedings of International Conference Defense Transformation and Net-Centric Systems 2008, as Part of the SPIE Defense and Security Symposium, World Center Marriott Resort and Convention Center, Orlando, FL, 16–20 March 2008 (Also: Proceedings of SPIE–Volume 6981, Defense Transformation and Net-Centric Systems 2008, Raja Suresh, Editor, 69810T, 3 April 2008).
14. P. S. Sapaty, Distributed Technology for Global Dominance. Keynote Lecture, Proceedings of the Fifth International Conference in Control, Automation and Robotics ICINCO 2008, The Conference Proceedings, Funchal, Madeira, 11–15 May 2008.
15. P. S. Sapaty, Human-Robotic Teaming: A Compromised Solution. AUVSI's Unmanned Systems North America, San Diego, CA, 10–12 June 2008.
16. P. S. Sapaty, High-Level Communication Protocol for Dynamically Networked Battlefields. Proceedings of International Conference Tactical Communications (Situational Awareness and Operational Effectiveness in the Last Tactical Mile), One Whitehall Place, Whitehall Suite and Reception, London, 2009.
17. P. S. Sapaty, Distributed Capability for Battlespace Dominance. Electronic Warfare 2009 Conference and Exhibition, Novotel London West Hotel and Conference Center, London, 14–15 May 2009.
18. P. S. Sapaty, Providing Spatial Integrity for Distributed Unmanned Systems. Proceedings of 6th International Conference in Control, Automation and Robotics ICINCO 2009, Milan, 2009.
19. P. S. Sapaty, Distributed Technology for Global Control. Book Chapter, Lecture Notes in Electrical Engineering, Informatics in Control, Automation and Robotics, Vol. 37. Berlin: Springer, 2009.
20. P. S. Sapaty, Gestalt-Based Integrity of Distributed Networked Systems. SPIE Europe Security + Defence. Berlin: BCC Berliner Congress Centre, 2009.
21. P. S. Sapaty, Remote Control of Open Groups of Remote Sensors. Proceedings of SPIE Europe Security + Defence, Berlin, 2009.
22. P. S. Sapaty, Tactical Communications in Advanced Systems for Asymmetric Operations. Proceedings of Tactical Communications, CCT Venues, Canary Wharf, London, 28–30 April 2010.
23. P. S. Sapaty, High-Level Technology to Manage Distributed Robotized Systems. Proceedings of Military Robotics, Jolly St Ermins, London, 25–27 May 2010.

24. P. S. Sapaty, Emerging Asymmetric Threats, Q&A Session. Tactical Communications, CCT Venues, Canary Wharf, London, 28–30 April 2010.
25. P. S. Sapaty, High-Level Organization and Management of Directed Energy Systems. Proceedings of Directed Energy Weapons, CCT, Canary Wharf, London, 25–26 March 2010.
26. P. S. Sapaty, Unified Transition to Robotized Armies with Spatial Grasp Technology, International Summit Military Robotics, London, 12–13 November 2012.
27. P. S. Sapaty, Distributed Air and Missile Defense with Spatial Grasp Technology, Intelligent Control and Automation, 2012, 3(2), 117–131.
28. P. S. Sapaty, Global Electronic Dominance. 12th International Fighter Symposium, Grand Connaught Rooms, London, 6–8 November 2012.
29. P. S. Sapaty, Providing Global Awareness in Distributed Dynamic Environments. International Summit ISR, London, 16–18 April 2013.
30. P. S. Sapaty, Ruling Distributed Dynamic Worlds with Spatial Grasp Technology. Tutorial at the International Science and Information Conference 2013 (SAI), London, 7–9 October 2013.
31. P. S. Sapaty, Night Vision Under Advanced Spatial Intelligence: A Key to Battlefield Dominance. International Summit Night Vision 2013, London, 4–6 June 2013.
32. P. S. Sapaty, Integration of ISR with Advanced Command and Control for Critical Mission Applications. SMi's ISR Conference, Holiday Inn Regents Park, London, 7–8 April 2014.
33. P. S. Sapaty, Unified Transition to Cooperative Unmanned Systems Under Spatial Grasp Paradigm, Transactions on Networks and Communications, 2014, 2(2).
34. P. S. Sapaty, From Manned to Smart Unmanned Systems: A Unified Transition. SMi's Military Robotics, Holiday Inn Regents Park, London, 21–22 May 2014.
35. P. S. Sapaty, Unified Transition to Cooperative Unmanned Systems Under Spatial Grasp Paradigm. 19th International Command and Control Research and Technology Symposium, Alexandria, VA, 16–19 June 2014.
36. P. S. Sapaty, Distributed Human Terrain Operations for Solving National and International Problems. International Relations and Diplomacy, 2014, 2(9).
37. P. S. Sapaty, Providing Over-Operability of Advanced ISR Systems by a High-Level Networking Technology. SMI's Airborne ISR, Holiday Inn Kensington Forum, London, 26–27 October 2015.
38. P. S. Sapaty, Distributed Missile Defence with Spatial Grasp Technology. SMi's Military Space, Holiday Inn Regents Park, London, 4–5 March 2015.
39. P. S. Sapaty, Military Robotics: Latest Trends and Spatial Grasp Solutions, International Journal of Advanced Research in Artificial Intelligence, 2015, 4(4).

40. P. S. Sapaty, A Brief Introduction to the Spatial Grasp Language (SGL), Journal of Computer Science & Systems Biology, 2015, 9(2). www.researchgate.net/publication/307744279_A_Brief_Introduction_to_the_Spatial_Grasp_Language_SGL

41. P. S. Sapaty, Organization of Advanced ISR Systems by High-level Networking Technology, Mathematical Machines and Systems, 2016, 1 (2016).

42. P. S. Sapaty, Towards Massively Robotized Systems Under Spatial Grasp Technology, Journal of Computer Science & Systems Biology, 2016, 9(1).

43. P. S. Sapaty, Towards Wholeness and Integrity of Distributed Dynamic Systems, Journal of Computer Science & Systems Biology, 2016, 9(3).

44. P. S. Sapaty, Towards Global Goal Orientation, Robustness and Integrity of Distributed Dynamic Systems, Journal of International Relations and Diplomacy, 2016, 4(6).

45. P. Sapaty, Spatial Grasp Language (SGL), Advances in Image and Video Processing, 2016, 4(1). https://journals.scholarpublishing.org/index.php/AIVP/article/view/1922/1052

46. P. S. Sapaty, Mosaic Warfare: From Philosophy to Model to Solution, Mathematical Machines and Systems, 2019, 3.

47. P. S. Sapaty, Global Network Management Under Spatial Grasp Paradigm, International Robotics & Automation Journal, 2020, 6(3), 134–148. https://medcraveonline.com/IRATJ/IRATJ-06-00212.pdf

48. P. S. Sapaty, Global Network Management Under Spatial Grasp Paradigm, Global Journal of Researches in Engineering, 2020, 20(5), Version 1.0, 58–81. https://globaljournals.org/GJRE_Volume20/6-Global-Network-Management.pdf

49. P. S. Sapaty, Advanced Terrestrial and Celestial Missions Under Spatial Grasp Technology, Aeronautics and Aerospace Open Access Journal, 2020, 4(3). https://medcraveonline.com/AAOAJ/AAOAJ-04-00110.pdf

50. P. S. Sapaty, Spatial Management of Distributed Social Systems, Journal of Computer Science Research, 2020, 2(3). https://ojs.bilpublishing.com/index.php/jcsr/article/view/2077/pdf

51. P. S. Sapaty, Towards Global Nanosystems Under High-level Networking Technology, Acta Scientific Computer Sciences, 2020, 2(8). www.actascientific.com/ASCS/pdf/ASCS-02-0051.pdf

52. P. S. Sapaty, Symbiosis of Distributed Simulation and Control Under Spatial Grasp Technology, SSRG International Journal of Mobile Computing and Application (IJMCA), 2020, 7(2). www.internationaljournalssrg.org/IJMCA/2020/Volume7-Issue2/IJMCA-V7I2P101.pdf

53. P. Sapaty, Symbiosis of Real and Simulated Worlds Under Global Awareness and Consciousness. Abstract at: The Science of Consciousness Conference, TSC, 14–18 September 2020. https://eagle.sbs.arizona.edu/sc/report_poster_detail.php?abs=3696

54. Đ. S. Sapaty, Spatial Grasp as a Model for Space-Based Control and Management Systems, Mathematical Machines and Systems, 2021, 1, 135–138. www.immsp.kiev.ua/publications/articles/2021/2021_1/Sapaty_book_1_2021.pdf

55. P. S. Sapaty, Managing Multiple Satellite Architectures by Spatial Grasp Technology, Mathematical Machines and Systems, 2021, 1, 3–16. www.immsp.kiev.ua/publications/eng/2021_1/

56. P. S. Sapaty, Spatial Management of Large Constellations of Small Satellites, Mathematical Machines and Systems, 2021, 2. www.immsp.kiev.ua/publications/articles/2021/2021_2/02_21_Sapaty.pdf

57. P. S. Sapaty, Global Management of Space Debris Removal Under Spatial Grasp Technology, Acta Scientific Computer Sciences, 2021, 3(7). www.actascientific.com/ASCS/pdf/ASCS-03-0135.pdf

58. P. S. Sapaty, Space Debris Removal Under Spatial Grasp Technology, Network and Communication Technologies, 2021, 6(1). www.ccsenet.org/journal/index.php/nct/article/view/0/45486

59. P. S. Sapaty, Relation of Spatial Grasp Paradigm to Higher Psychological and Mental Concepts, Acta Scientific Computer Sciences, 2022, 4(12). https://actascientific.com/ASCS/pdf/ASCS-04-0359.pdf

60. P. S. Sapaty, Seeing and Managing Distributed Worlds with Spatial Grasp Paradigm, Acta Scientific Computer Sciences, 2022, 4(12). https://actascientific.com/ASCS/pdf/ASCS-04-0365.pdf

61. P. S. Sapaty, Comprehending Distributed Worlds with the Spatial Grasp Paradigm, Mathematical Machines and Systems, 2022, 1. www.immsp.kiev.ua/publications/articles/2022/2022_1/01_22_Sapaty.pdf

62. P. S. Sapaty, Spatial Management of Air and Missile Defence Operations, Mathematical Machines and Systems, 2023, 1. www.immsp.kiev.ua/publications/articles/2023/2023_1/01_23_Sapaty.pdf

63. P. S. Sapaty, Providing Distributed System Integrity under Spatial Grasp Technology, Mathematical Machines and Systems, 2023, 2. www.immsp.kiev.ua/publications/articles/2023/2023_2/02_23_Sapaty.pdf

64. P. S. Sapaty, Providing Global Awareness in Distributed Dynamic Systems, International Relations and Diplomacy, 2023, 11(2), 87–100. https://doi.org/10.17265/2328-2134/2023.02.002. www.davidpublisher.com/Public/uploads/Contribute/6486c3d05a6cc.pdf

65. P. S. Sapaty, Simulating Distributed Consciousness with Spatial Grasp Model, Mathematical Machines and Systems, 2023, 3.

66. P. S. Sapaty, Managing Distributed Systems with Spatial Grasp Patterns, Mathematical Machines and Systems, 2023, 4.

67. Mobile Agent. https://en.wikipedia.org/wiki/Mobile_agent

68. Telescript Language Reference, General Magic, October 1995. http://bitsavers.informatik.uni-stuttgart.de/pdf/generalMagic/Telescript_Language_Reference_Oct95.pdf

69. A. T. Bondarenko, S. B. Mikhalevich, A. I. Nikitin, P. S. Sapaty, Software of BESM-6 Computer for Communication with Peripheral Computers via Telephone Channels. In Computer Software, Vol. 5. Kiev: Institute of Cybernetics Press, 1970.

70. P. S. Sapaty, A Method of Organization of an Intercomputer Dialogue in the Radial Computer Systems. In The Design of Software and Hardware for Automatic Control Systems. Kiev: Institute of Cybernetics Press, 1973.

71. P. S. Sapaty, A Wave Language for Parallel Processing of Semantic Networks, Computing and Artificial Intelligence, 1986, 5(4), 289–314.
72. P. S. Sapaty, Distributed Modeling of Cooperative Behavior by Mobile Agents. Proceedings of the Sixth Conference on Computer Generated Forces and Behavioral Representation, IST UCF, Orlando, FL, July 1996, pp. 599–613.

3

SPATIAL GRASP
LANGUAGE DETAILS

3.1 Introduction

This chapter provides full details on Spatial Grasp Language, which may be particularly useful for proper understanding of numerous practical examples of the use of SGL code in the subsequent chapters. More information on SGL can be obtained in [1–14], as well as from previous language versions called WAVE [15–37]. The rest of the chapter is organized as follows. Section 3.2 describes different types of SGL constants, which can be self-identifiable by the way they are written or generally defined by special rules. These include information, physical matter, special constants, compound constants, and custom constants. Section 3.3 describes different types of SGL variables with their semantics, spatial distribution, and movement, which include global variables, heritable variables, frontal variables, nodal variables, and environmental variables. Section 3.4 provides the full repertoire of SGL rules with their semantics and practical use, which include type, usage, movement, creation, echoing, verification, assignment, advancement, branching, transference, exchange, timing, qualification, and grasping. Section 3.5 summarizes the full SGL syntax, and Section 3.6 concludes the chapter.

3.2 SGL Constants

Constants can be self-identifiable by the way they are written, as follows, or defined by special rules embracing them with arbitrary textual representations.

- **Information**

A *string* can be represented as a sequence of characters embraced by opening and closing single quotation marks:

 DOI: 10.1201/9781003425267-3

`'{character}'`

This sequence can contain other single quotes only if they appear in opening-closing pairs, with such nesting allowed to any depth. If single words representing information do not intersect with other language constructs, the quotes can be omitted.

Another string representation may be an *explicit SGL scenario body*, where the sequence of characters should be placed into opening-closing braces, shown next in bold to distinguish from braces for textual repetition in the language syntax:

`{{character}}`

Braces will indicate the text as a potential *scenario* code that should be optimized *before* its usage.

Number can be represented in a standard way, similar to traditional programming languages, generally in the following form (with brackets identifying optional parts and braces the repeating characters).

`[sign]{digit}[.{digit}[E[sign]{digit}]]`

- **Physical matter**

Physical *matter* (physical objects included) in the most general way can be reflected in SGL by a sequence of characters embraced by opening-closing double quotation marks:

`"{character}"`

- **Special constants**

These include the following.

thru—indicates (or artificially sets up) a control state of the scenario in the current world point as an *absolute success* with possibility of further scenario evolution from this particular point.

done—indicates (or artificially sets up) a control state as a *successful termination* in the current world point, blocking further scenario development from this particular point.

fail—indicates (or artificially sets up) a scenario control state as a *failure* in the current world point, without the possibility of further scenario development from this particular point.

fatal—indicates (or artificially sets up) a control state as nonlocal *fatal failure* starting in the current world point and causing massive termination and removal of all active distributed processes with related data in this and other world points reached by the same scenario. The destructive influence of this state may be contained at higher levels by special rules.

infinite—indicates infinitely large value.

nil—indicates no value at all.

any, all, other, allother—stating that *any one*, *all* (the current one including), *any other*, or *all other* elements can be considered and used by some rule.

current—refers to the current element (like a node) only, for its further consideration or reentering.

passed—informing that the mentioned elements (like world nodes) have already been passed by the current branch to the current point. They may be accessed easier by backwarding via the history-based distributed control than by a global search.

existing—hinting that world nodes with the given names already exist and should not be created again.

neighbors—stating that the nodes to be accessed are among direct neighbors of the current node, i.e. within a single hop from via existing links.

direct—stating that the mentioned nodes should be accessed or created from the current node directly, without considering semantic links to them (even if such links may already exist).

forward, backward, neutral—allowing control to move from the current node via existing links along, against, or regardless their orientations (non-oriented links can always be traversed in both directions).

synchronous, asynchronous—a modifier setting synchronous or asynchronous mode of operations.

virtual, physical, executive—indicating or setting the type of a node the scenario is currently dealing with (the node can also be of a combined type).

engaged, vacant—indicating or setting the state of a resource the current scenario is dealing with.

firstcome—allows the current scenario with its unique identity to enter the world nodes only the first time (the capability based on internal node marking mechanisms).

unique—allows the return of only unique elements received from the embraced scenario's final positions while omitting duplicates.

- **Compound constants**

Constants can also be compound ones, using the recursive *grasp* definition in SGL syntax that allows us to represent nested hierarchical structures consisting of multiple (elementary or compound again) objects. This, in particular for constants, can be expressed as:

rule ({*constant*,})

- **Custom constants**

Other self-identifiable, or *custom*, constants can be incorporated to be directly processed by updated SGL, if they do not conflict with the language syntax; otherwise, they should be declared by special rules.

3.3 SGL Variables

- **Global variables**

These are the most expensive type of SGL variables, with their names starting with capital G and followed by arbitrary sequences of alphabetic letters and/or digits:

G{*alphameric*}

These variables can exist only in single copies with particular names, being common for both read and write operations to all processes of the same scenario, regardless of their physical or virtual distribution and world points they may cover.

- **Heritable variables**

The names of these variables should start with capital H if not defined by a special rule:

H{*alphameric*}

Heritable variables, being created by first assignment to them at some scenario development stage, are becoming common for read-write operations *for all subsequent* scenario operations (generally multiple, parallel, and distributed) evolving from this particular point and wherever space may happen to be. This means that such variables are unique only within concrete hereditary scenario developments, to all their depth.

- **Frontal variables**

These are mobile type variables with names starting with capital F, which propagate in distributed spaces while keeping their contents on the forefronts of evolving scenarios:

F{*alphameric*}

Each of these variables serves only the current scenario branch operating in the current world point. They cannot be shared with other branches evolving in the same or other world points, while always accompanying the scenario control. If the scenario splits into individual branches, these variables are replicated with the same names and contents and serve these branches independently.

- **Nodal variables**

Variables of this type, their identifiers starting with capital N, are a temporary and exclusive property of the world points visited by SGL scenarios, which can create, change, or remove them.

N{*alphameric*}

Capable of being shared by all scenario branches visiting these nodes, they are created by first assignment to them and stay in the node until removed explicitly or the whole scenario remains active. These variables also cease to exist when the nodes they associate with are removed by any scenario reaching them.

- **Environmental variables**

These are special variables with reserved names (all in capitals) that allow us to have access to physical, virtual, and executive worlds when they are navigated by SGL scenarios, as well as to some parameters of the language interpretation system itself.

TYPE—indicates the type of a node the current scenario step associates with and returns a verbal expression of the node's type (i.e. `virtual`, `physical`, `executive`, or their combination). It can also change the existing node's type by assigning to it another value (simple or combined).

NAME—returns the name of the current node as a string of characters (only if the node has a virtual or an executive dimension or both). Assigning to this variable when staying in the node can change the node's name.

CONTENT—returns the content of the current node (if it has a virtual or an executive dimension or both) as any text, vector, or nested structure of multiple texts, etc. Assigning to this variable when staying in the node can set up or change the node's content.

ADDRESS—returns a unique address of the node having virtual dimension. This is a read-only variable, as node addresses are set up automatically by the underlying distributed SGL interpretation system during the node's creation or by an external system (like the internet address of the node).

QUALITIES—identifies a list of selected formalized physical parameters associated with the current physical position, or node, depending on the chosen implementation and application (for example, these may be temperature, humidity, air pressure, visibility, radiation, noise or pollution level, density, salinity, etc.). These parameters (generally as a list of values) can be obtained by reading the variable, and some can be changed, influencing the world from its particular point.

WHERE—keeps world coordinates of the current physical node (or the one having physical dimension too) in the chosen coordinate system. These coordinates can be obtained by reading this variable. Assigning a new value to this variable (with possible speed added) can cause physical movement into the new position.

BACK—keeps an internal system link to the preceding world node (virtual, executive, or combined), allowing the scenario to most efficiently return to the previously occupied node, if needed.

PREVIOUS—refers to the absolute and unique address of the previous virtual node (or a combined one with executive and/or physical dimensions), allowing us to return to the node directly. Its content, unlike with BACK, can be lifted, recorded, and used elsewhere in the scenario (but not changed).

PREDECESSOR—refers to the name of preceding world node (the one with virtual or executive dimension, visited just before the current one). Its content can be lifted, recorded, and subsequently used, for organization of direct hops to this node too (on most expensive level, however).

DOER—keeps the name of the device (say, laptop, robot, satellite, smart sensor, or a specially equipped human), which interprets the current SGL code in the current world position. This device can be initially chosen for the scenario automatically from the list of recommended devices or just picked up from those expected available. It can also be appointed explicitly by assigning its name to DOER.

RESOURCES—may keep a list of available or recommended resources (human, robotic, electronic, mechanical etc., by their types or names) that can be used for planning and execution of the current and subsequent parts of the SGL scenario. This list can also contain potential doers that may appear (by their names) in variables DOER.

LINK—keeps the name (same as content) of the virtual link that has just been passed. Assigning a new value to it can change the link's content/name. Assigning nil or empty to LINK removes the link passed.

DIRECTION—keeps direction (along, against, or neutral) of the passed virtual link. Assigning to this variable values like plus, minus, or nil (same as +, -, or empty) can change its orientation or make the link non-oriented.

WHEN—assigning value to this variable sets up an absolute starting time for the following scenario branch (i.e. starting with the next operation), thus allowing us to suspend and schedule operations and their groups in time.

TIME—returns the current absolute system time as the read-only global variable.

STATE—can be used for explicit setting resultant control state of the current scenario step by assigning to it one of the following constants: thru, done, fail, or fatal, which will influence further scenario development from the current world point (and in a broader scale in the case of fatal). These control states are also generated implicitly and automatically on the results of success or failure of different operations (belonging to the internal interpretation mechanisms of SGL scenarios). Reading STATE will always return thru, as this could be possible only if the previous operation terminated with thru too, thus letting this operation proceed.

VALUE—when accessed, returns the resultant value of the latest, i.e. preceding, operation (say, an assignment to it or any other variable, unassigned result of arithmetic or string operation, or just naming a variable or constant).

IDENTITY—keeps identity, or color, of the current SGL scenario or its branch, which propagates together with the scenario and influences grouping of different nodal variables under this identity at world nodes reached. This allows different scenarios or their branches with personal identities to be protected from influencing each other, even if they are using the same named nodal variables in the same world nodes.

IN—special variable requesting and reading data from the outside world in its current point. The received data is becoming the resultant value of the reading operation.

OUT—special variable allowing us to issue information from the scenario in its current point to the outside world, by assigning the output value to this variable.

STATUS—retrieving or setting the status of (especially doer) node in which the scenario is currently staying (like engaged or vacant, possibly, with a numerical estimate of the level of engagement or vacancy). This feedback from implementation layer on the SGL scenario layer can be useful for a higher-level supervision, planning, and distribution of resources executing the scenario rather than doing this implicitly and automatically.

3.4 SGL Rules

• **Type rules**

These rules explicitly assign types to different constructs, with their existing repertoire following.

> **global, heritable, frontal, nodal, environmental**—allow different types of variables to have any alphanumeric names rather than those oriented on self-identification, as explained before. These names will represent variables with needed types in the subsequent scenario developments unless redefined by these rules too.
>
> **matter, number, string, scenario, constant**—allow arbitrary results obtained by the embraced scenario to properly represent the needed values rather than using self-identifiable representations mentioned before.

• **Usage rules**

These rules explain how to use the information units they embrace.

> **address**—identifies the embraced value (which may also be arbitrary scenario producing this value) as an address of a virtual node.
>
> **coordinate**—identifies the embraced value as physical coordinates (say, one, two, or three dimensional).
>
> **content**—identifies the embraced operand as a content (or contents).
>
> **index**—identifies the embraced operand as an index (or indices) that may represent orders of elements in a list for its search by the index operation.
>
> **time**—informs that the embraced operand represents time value.
>
> **speed**—informs that the embraced operand represents a value of speed.
>
> **name**—identifies the embraced operand as a name (say, of a virtual or executive node or nodes).
>
> **center**—depending on applications, indicates that virtual address or physical coordinates embraced may relate to the center of some region.

range—identifies virtual or physical distance that can, for example, be used as a threshold for certain operations in distributed spaces, especially those evolving from a chosen or expected center.

doer—identifies the embraced name or any other value as belonging to executive node (like human, robot, server, satellite, smart phone, etc.).

node—(or **nodes**, if more appropriate) identifies the embraced value or values as keeping names of nodes having virtual or/ and executive dimensions.

link—(or **links**, when more appropriate) informs that the embraced value or values represent names of links connecting nodes.

- **Movement rules**

These rules may result in virtual hopping to the existing nodes (the ones having virtual or/and executive dimensions) or in real movement to new physical locations, subsequently starting the remaining scenario if any (with current frontal variables and control) in the nodes reached. See movement examples, detailed and explained later, in Figure 3.1.

hop—sets electronic propagation to a node (or nodes) in virtual, executive, or combined spaces (the latter may have physical dimension too) directly or via semantic links connecting them with the starting node. In the case of a direct hop, except destination node name or address, special modifier direct may be included into parameters of the rule. If the hop is to take place from a node to a particular node via an existing link, both destination node name/address and link name (with orientation if appropriate) should be parameters of the rule.

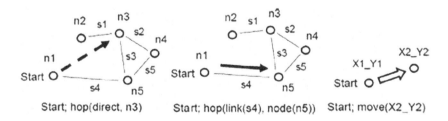

Start; hop(direct, n3)   Start; hop(link(s4), node(n5))   Start; move(X2_Y2)

Figure 3.1   Examples of movement in SGL.

hopfirst—modification of the hop rule allowing it to come to a node only the first time (for the scenario with certain identity), which is based on an internal interpretation mechanism marking the nodes visited.

hopforth—modification of the previous rule allowing it to hop to a node that is not the one just visited before, i.e. excluding the return to the previous node. It may be considered as a restricted variant of the hopfirst rule.

move—sets real movement in the physical world from the current node with physical dimension (which may be combined with virtual and executive ones) to a particular location given by coordinates in a chosen coordinate system. Speed value for the physical propagation by move may be given as an additional parameter.

shift—differs from the move only in that movement in physical world is set by deviations of physical coordinates from the current position rather than by their absolute values.

follow—allows us to move in virtual, physical, and combined spaces using already recorded and saved paths from a starting node to the destinations reached, to enter the latter again.

• **Creation rules**

These rules create or remove nodes and/or links leading to them during distributed world navigation. After termination of the creation rules, their resultant values will correspond to the names of reached nodes with termination states thru in them, and the next scenario's steps, if any, will start from all these nodes. If the creation or removal operation fails, its resultant value will be nil and control state fail in the node the rule started. Related creative examples are in Figure 3.2.

create—starting in the current world position, creates either new virtual link-node pairs or new isolated nodes. For the first case, the rule is supplied with names and orientations

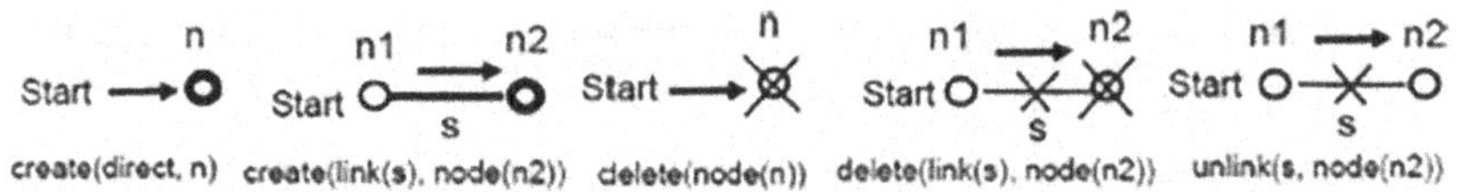

Figure 3.2 Creation and removal of nodes and/or links.

of new links and names of the new nodes these links should lead to, which may be multiple. For the second case, the rule has to use the modifier `direct` indicating direct node creation.

linkup—restricts the previous rule by creating only links with proper names from the current node to the already existing nodes given by their names or addresses.

delete—starting from the current node, removes links together with the nodes they should lead to. Links and nodes to be removed should be either explicitly named or represented by modifiers `any` or `all`. Using the modifier `direct` will allow us to remove such a node (or nodes) from the current node directly.

unlink—removes only links leading to neighboring nodes where, similar to the previous case, they should be explicitly named; otherwise, the modifiers `any` or `all` are used instead.

- **Echoing rules**

This class of rules, oriented on various aspects of data and knowledge processing, contains the following rules that may use local and remote values for different operations. The listed rules use terminal world positions reached by the embraced scenario with their control states and associated final values (which may be local or arbitrarily remote) to obtain the resultant state and value in the location where the rule started. See echoing scenario scheme example in Figure 3.3.

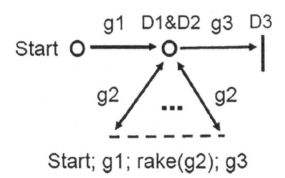

Figure 3.3 with the echo rule inside:

g1 D1&D2 g3 D3

Start O———→O———→|

g2 / ... \ g2

Start; g1; rake(g2); g3

Figure 3.3 Scenario example with the echo rule.

state—returns the resultant generalized state of the embraced SGL scenario upon its completion, whatever its complexity and space coverage may be. This state is the result of ascending fringe-to-root generalization of terminal states of the scenario embraced, where states with higher power (their sequence from maximum to minimum values: fatal, thru, done, fail) dominate in this potentially distributed and parallel process.

rake—returns a list of final values of the scenario embraced in arbitrary order, which may, for example, be influenced by the order of completion of branches and times of reaching their final destinations. Additionally, when using unique as a modifier, described before, the rule will result in collecting only unique values.

order—returns an ordered list of final values of the scenario embraced corresponding to the order of launching related branches rather than the order of their completion. For potentially parallel branches, these orders may, for example, relate to how they were activated, possibly with the use of time stamps upon invocation.

unit—returns a list of values while arranging it as an integral parenthesized unit which should not be mixed with elements returned from other branches that may represent integral units too, to form (potentially hierarchical and nested) lists of lists of the obtained values at higher levels.

sum—returns the sum of all final values of the scenario embraced.

count—returns the number of all resultant values associated with the scenario embraced.

first, last, min, max, random, average—return, correspondingly, the first, last, minimum, maximum, randomly chosen, or average value from all terminal values returned by the scenario embraced.

sortup, sortdown—return an ordered list of values produced by the embraced scenario operand, starting from minimum or maximum value and ending, correspondingly, with the maximum or minimum one.

reverse—changes to the opposite order of values from the embraced operand.

element—returns the value of an element of the list on its left operand requested by index or content given by the right operand. If the right operand is itself a list of indices or contents, the result will be the list of corresponding values from the left operand. If element is used within the left operand of assignment, instead of returning values it will provide access to them in order to be updated.

position—returns the index (or indices) of the list on its left operand requested by the content given by the right operand. There may be more than a single index returned if the same content repeats in the list, or if the right operand is itself a list of contents.

fromto—returns an ordered list of digital values by naming its first (operand 1) and last (operand 2) elements as well as step value (operand 3), allowing the next element to be obtained from the previous one. Another modification (depending on implementation) may take into account the starting element, step value, and the number of needed elements in the list.

add, subtract, multiply, divide, degree—perform corresponding operations on two or more operands embraced, each potentially represented by an arbitrary scenario with local or remote results. If the operands themselves provide multiple values, as lists, these operations are performed between peer elements of these lists, with the resultant value as a list too.

separate—separates the left operand string value by the string at the right operand used as a delimiter in a repeated manner for the left string, with the result being the list of separated substring values. If the right operand is a list of delimiters, its elements will be used sequentially and cyclically unless the string at the left is fully processed/partitioned.

unite—integrates the list of values at the left (as strings, or to be converted into strings automatically) by a repeated delimiter as a string too (or a cyclically used list of them) at the right into a united string.

attach—produces the resultant string by connecting the right string operand directly to the end of the left one. If operands are lists with more than one element, the attachment is made between their peer elements, receiving the resultant list of united strings. This rule can also operate with more than two operands.

append—forms the resultant list from left and right operands by appending the latter to the end of the former as individual elements, where both operands may be lists themselves. More than two operands can also be used for this operation.

common—returns the intersection of two or more lists as operands, with the result including only the same elements of all lists, if any.

withdraw—its returned result will be the first element of the list provided by the embraced operand, along with withdrawing this element from the head of the list (thus simultaneously changing the content of the variable). This rule can have another operand providing the number of elements to be withdrawn in one step and represented as the result.

increment—adds 1 (one) to the value of the embraced operand, which will be the result on this rule, thus simultaneously changing the content of the operand itself. If another value, not 1, is added, the second operand can keep this value.

decrement—behaves similar to the previous rule `increment` but subtracts rather than adds 1 from the value of the embraced operand, with the content of the latter simultaneously changed. A second operand can be used if the value to subtract does not equal 1.

access—by embracing a scenario or its branch, it returns a reference to the internal history-based optimized and recorded structure leading from the rule-activation node to the reached terminal nodes. This reference can be remembered (say, in a variable) and subsequently used from the same starting node for reaching exactly the same terminal nodes again.

invert—changes the sign of a value or orientation of a link to the opposite, while producing no effect on zero values or non-oriented links.

`apply`—organizes the application of the first operand as one or a set of rules described earlier operating jointly from the same starting point to the same second scenario operand, which may be arbitrary. If multiple application rules engaged on the first operand, the obtained results on the second operand can be multiple too.

`location`—returns world locations of the final nodes reached by the embraced scenario, which means for virtual nodes their network addresses and for physical nodes their physical coordinates.

`distance`—returns distance between two physical points defined by absolute physical coordinates expressed by its parameters, where each one can be represented by an arbitrary scenario.

- **Verification rules**

These rules provide control state `thru` or `fail` reflecting the result of concrete verification procedure, also `nil` as its own resultant value, while remaining after completion in the same world positions where they started.

`equal, nonequal, less, lessorequal, more, moreorequal, bigger, smaller, heavier, lighter, longer, shorter`—make corresponding comparison between left and right operands, which can represent information or physical matter/objects, or both. In case of vector operands, state `thru` appears only if all peer values satisfy the condition set up by the rule (except `nonequal`, for which even a single non-correspondence between any peers will result in overall `thru`).

`empty, nonempty`—checks for emptiness (i.e. non-existence of anything, same as `nil`) or non-emptiness (existence) of the resultant value obtained from the embraced scenario.

`belong, notbelong`—verifies whether the left operand value (single or a list with all its elements) belongs as a whole to the right operand generally represented as a list (which may have a single element too).

`intersect, notintersect`—verifies whether there are common elements (values) in the left and right operands, considered generally as lists. More than two operands can be used for these rules too, with at least a single same element to be present in all of them to result `thru` for `intersect`, or no such elements for `notintersect`.

yes—verifies generalized state of the embraced scenario providing own control state `thru` in case of `thru` or `done` from the entire scenario, and control state fail in case of resultant `fail` or `fatal` (thus allowing to continue from the node where the rule started only in case of success of the embraced scenario).

no—verifies generalized state of the embraced scenario resulting with own control state `thru` in case of `fail` or `fatal` from the scenario, and control state `fail` in case of `thru` or `done` (i.e. allowing to continue from the rule's starting node only in case of failure of the embraced scenario).

- **Assignment rules**

These rules assign the result of the right scenario operand (which may be arbitrarily remote and also represent a list of values that can be nested) to the variable or set of variables directly named or reached by the left scenario operand, which may be remote too. The left operand can also provide pointers to certain elements of the reached variables that should be changed by the assignment rather than the whole contents of variables.

assign—assigns the same value of the right operand (which may be a list of values) to all values (like, say, node names) or variables accessed by the left operand (or their particular elements pointed, which may themselves become lists after assignment, thus extending the lists of contents of these variables). If the right operand is `nil` or empty, the left operand nodes or variables as a whole (or only their certain elements pointed) will be removed.

assignpeers—assigns values of different elements of the list on the right operand to different values or variables (or their pointed elements) associated with the destinations reached on the left operand, in a peer-to-peer mode.

• **Advancement rules**

These rules can organize forward or "in depth" advancement in space and time of the embraced scenarios separated by comma. They can evolve within their sequence in synchronous or asynchronous mode using modifiers `synchronous` or `asynchronous` (the second one is optional, as asynchronous is a default mode).

`advance`—organizes stepwise scenario advancement in physical, virtual, executive, or combined spaces, as well as in a pure computational space (the latter when staying in the same world nodes with certain data processing, thus moving in time only). For this, the embraced SGL scenario operands are used in a sequence, as written, where each new scenario shifts to and applies from all terminal world points reached by the previous scenario. The resultant world positions and values on the whole rule are associated with the final steps of the last scenario on the rule. And the rule's resultant state is a generalization of control states associated with these final steps.

`slide`—works similar to the previous rule unless a scenario in its sequence fails to produce resultant state `thru` or `done` from some world node. In this case the next scenario from the sequence will be applied from the same starting position of the previous, failed, scenario and so on. The resultant world nodes and values in them will be from the last successfully applied scenarios (not necessarily the same from their sequence, as independently developing in different directions).

`repeat`—invokes the embraced scenario as many times as possible, with each new iteration taking place in parallel from all final positions with state `thru` reached by the previous invocations. If some scenario iteration fails, its current starting position with its value will be included into the set of final positions and values on the whole rule (this set may have starting positions from different failed iterations which developed independently in a distributed space). By supplying an additional numeric modifier to this rule, it is possible to explicitly limit the number of allowed scenario repetitions. Some examples of the development of the latest three rules are shown in Figure 3.4.

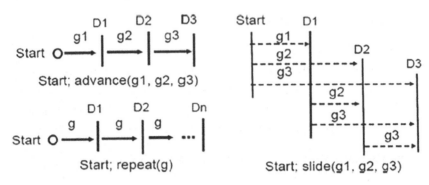

Figure 3.4   Scenario examples for advancement rules.

align—is based on confirmation of full termination of all activities of the embraced operand scenario in all its final nodes. Only after this, the remaining scenario part, if any, will be allowed to continue from all the nodes reached.

fringe—allows us to establish certain constraints (say, by additional parameters) on the terminal world nodes reached by the embraced scenario with final values in them, to be considered as starting positions for the following scenario parts. For example, by comparing values in all terminal nodes and allowing the scenario to continue from a node with maximum or minimum value, integrating this rule with previously mentioned rules max or min like **max _ fringe** or **min _ fringe** can also be possible.

For the advancement rules, frontal variables propagate on the forefronts together with advancement of control and operations in distributed spaces, with next scenarios or their iterations picking up frontal variables brought to their starting points by the previous scenarios, being also replicated if this control automatically splits into different branches.

- **Branching rules**

These rules allow the embraced set of scenario operands to develop "in breadth," each from the same starting position, with the resultant set of positions and order of their appearance depending on the logic of a concrete branching rule. The rest of the SGL scenario will develop from all or some of the positions and nodes reached on the rule. The branching may be static and explicit if we have a clear set of individual operand scenarios separated by comma. It can also be implicit and dynamic, as explained later. For all branching rules that follow, the frontal variables associated with the rule's starting position will be replicated together with their contents and used independently within different branches. An example of a scenario with branching rule is shown in Figure 3.5.

branch—the most general and neutral variant of branching, with logical independence of the scenario operands from each other and any possible order of their invocation and development from the starting position. The resultant set of positions reached with their associated values will unite all terminal positions and values on all scenario operands involved under branch. The resultant control state on the whole rule will be based on generalization of the generalized control states on all scenario branches.

sequence—organizing strictly sequential invocation of all scenario operands regardless of their success or failure, and launching the next scenario only after full completion of the previous one. The resultant set of positions, values, and the rule's global control state will be similar to branch. However, the final results may vary due to different invocation order of the scenario operands and possible common information used.

parallel—organizing fully parallel development of all scenario operands from the same starting position. The resultant

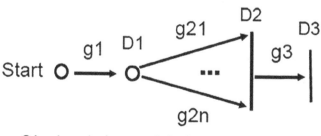

Start; g1; branch(g21,.., g2n); g3

Figure 3.5 The use of branching rule.

set of positions, values, and the rule's control state will be
similar to the previous two rules, but may not be the same, as
explained before.

if—may have three scenario operands. If the *first* scenario
results in the generalized termination state thru or done,
the *second* scenario is activated, otherwise the *third* one will be
launched. The resultant set of positions and associated values
will be the same as achieved by the second or third scenarios
after their completion. If the third operand scenario is absent
and the first one results in fail, or only the first operand is
present regardless of its success or failure, the resultant position will be the one the rule started from, with state thru
and value it had at the start.

or—allows *only one* operand scenario with the resulting state
thru or done, without any predetermined order of their
invocation, to be registered as resultant, with the final positions and associated values on it to be the resulting ones on the
whole rule. The activities of all other scenario operands and
all results produced by them will be terminated and cancelled.

orsequence—will launch the scenario operands in strictly
sequential manner, one after the other as they are written,
waiting for their full completion before activating the next
operand, unless the first one in the sequence replies with the
generalized state thru or done (providing the result on
the rule as a whole). Invocation of the remaining scenarios
in the sequence will be skipped.

orparallel—activates all scenario operands in parallel from
the same current position, with the first one in time replying with a generalized thru or done being registered as the
resultant branch for the rule. All other branches will be forcefully terminated without waiting for their completion (or just
ignored).

and—activates all scenario operands from the same position,
without any predetermined order, demanding all of them
to return the generalized states thru or done. If at least
a single operand returns a generalized fail, the whole rule
results with state fail and nil value in the starting position

while terminating the development of all other branches that may still be in progress. If all operand scenarios succeed, the resulting set of positions unites all resultant positions on all scenario operands with their associated values.

andsequence—activates scenario operands from the same position in the written order, launching the next scenario only after the previous one completes with thru or done and terminating the whole rule when the current scenario results with fail. The remaining scenario operands will be ignored, and all results produced by this and all previous operands will be removed.

andparallel—activates in parallel all scenario operands from the same world position, terminating the rule when the first one in time results with fail, while aborting activity of all other operands and removing all results produced by the rule.

choose—chooses a scenario branch in their sequence *before* its execution, using additional parameters among which, for example, may be its numerical order in the sequence (or a list of such orders to select more than one branch). This rule can also be aggregated with other rules like first, last, or random, by forming combined ones: **choose _ first, choose _ last, choose _ random**.

quickest—selects the first branch in time replying its complete termination, regardless of its generalized termination state, which may happen to be fail too, even though other branches (to be forcefully terminated now) could respond later with thru or done. The state, set of positions on this selected branch, and their associated values (if any) will be taken as those for the whole rule. This rule assumes that different branches are launched independently and in parallel.

cycle—repeatedly invokes the embraced scenario from the same starting position until its resultant generalized state remains thru or done, where on different invocations the same or different sets of resultant positions (with same or different values) may emerge. The resultant set of positions on the whole rule will be an integration of all positions on all successful scenario invocations with their associated values. The following scenario will develop from all these world positions reached.

loop—differs from the previous rule in that the resultant set of positions on it is only the set produced by the *last* successful invocation of the embraced scenario.

sling—invokes repeatedly the embraced scenario until it provides state thru or done, always resulting in the same starting position with state thru and its previously associated value.

whirl—endlessly repeating the embraced scenario from the starting position regardless of its success or failure and ignoring any resultant positions or values produced. External forceful termination of this construct may be needed, like using first in time termination of another, competitive, branch.

split—performs, if needed, additional (and deeper than usual) static or dynamic partitioning of the embraced scenario into different branches, especially in complex and not clear at first sight cases, all starting from the same current position. It may be used alone or in combination with the aforementioned branching rules while preparing separate branches for these rules, ahead of their invocation.

replicate—replicates the scenario given by its second operand, providing the number of its copies given by the first operand, with each copy behaving as an independent branch starting from the same current world position.

• **Transference rules**

These rules organize transference of control in distributed scenarios.

run—transfers control to the SGL code treated as a procedure and being a result of invocation of the embraced scenario. The procedure (or a list of them) obtained and activated in such a way can produce a set of world positions with associated values and control states as the result on the rule, similar to other rules.

call—transfers control to the code produced by the embraced scenario that may represent activation of external systems. The resultant world position on call will be the same where the rule started, with value in it of what has been returned from the external call and state `thru` if the call was successful.

- **Exchange rules**

These rules include the following.

`input`—provides input of external information or physical matter (objects) on the initiative of SGL scenario, resulting in the same position but with value received from the outside. The rule may have an additional argument clarifying a particular external source from which the input should take place.

`output`—outputs the resultant value obtained by the embraced scenario, which can be multiple, with the same resultant position as before and associated value sent outside (in case of physical matter, the resultant value may depend on the applications). The rule may have an additional pointer to a particular external sink.

`send`—staying in the current position associated with physical, virtual, or executive (or combined) node; sends information or matter obtained by the scenario on the first operand to other similar node given by name, address, or coordinates provided by the second operand, assuming that a companion rule `receive` is already engaged there. The rule may have an additional parameter setting an acceptable time delay for the consumption of this data at the receiving end.

`receive`—a companion to rule `send`, naming the source of data to be received from (defined similarly to the destination node in `send`). Additional timing (as a second operand) may be set too, after expiration of which the rule will be considered as failed. In case of successful receipt of the data, the rule will result in the same world position and the value obtained.

`emit`—depending on implementation and technical capabilities, can trigger nonlocal to global continuous broadcasting of the data obtained by the embraced scenario, possibly with tagging of this source (also setting the emission frequency). Another operand providing time allowed for this broadcasting may be present too. No feedback from possible consumers of the sent data is expected.

`get`—tries to receive data which can be broadcast from some source (say, identified by its tag or frequency), with resultant value as the received data and state `thru`. No synchronization with the data-emitting node is expected.

- **Timing rules**

These rules deal with conditions related to a time interval for the scenarios they embrace.

`sleep`—establishes time delay defined by the embraced scenario operand, with suspending activities of this particular scenario branch in the current node. The rule's starting position and its existing value, also state `thru`, will be the result on the rule after the time passed.

`allowed`—sets time limit by the first operand for an activity of the scenario on the second operand. If the scenario terminates before expiration of this time frame, its resultant positions with values and states will define the result on this rule. Otherwise the scenario will be forcibly aborted.

- **Qualification rules**

These rules provide certain qualities or abilities and also set constraints or restrictions to the scenarios they embrace, as follows.

`contain`—restricts the spread of abortive consequences caused by control state `fatal` within the ruled scenario. This state may appear automatically and accidentally at different scenario development points or can be assigned explicitly to environmental variable `STATE`, triggering emergent completion of multiple scenario processes and removal of temporary data associated with them. The resultant position on the rule `contain` having state `fatal` inside its scenario will be the one it started from, with value `nil` and state `fail`.

`release`—allows the embraced scenario to develop free from the main scenario, abandoning bilateral control links with it (the main scenario after the rule's activation "will not see" this construct any more). The released, now independent, scenario will develop in a usual way using its standard subordination and control mechanisms.

trackless—allows the whole embraced scenario to develop absolutely free from any previous stages (i.e. without saving any control and information links with them) like a real virus, being an extreme and global variant of release. Under this rule, frontal variables carrying information between different stages will work as usual.

free—differs from the previous case in that despite its independence and control freedom from the main scenario, as before, the embraced scenario will nevertheless be obliged to return the final data obtained in its terminal positions to the main scenario.

blind, quit, abort—after full completion of the embraced scenario, these rules result in the same position the rule started with respective states done, fail, or fatal, thus preventing further scenario development from this point (also triggering nonlocal termination and cancellation processes in case of fatal).

stay—whatever the scenario embraced and its evolution in space, the resultant position will always be the same this rule started from, with value nil and state thru in it. If the ruled scenario is omitted, this rule standing alone just represents an empty operation at the current point, which can also be used for declaring a new scenario branch.

lift—lifts blocking of the further scenario developments set up by states done in the embraced scenario wherever it happened to emerge, substituting them with thru and allowing further developments from all such positions.

seize—establishes, or seizes, an absolute control over the resources associated with the current virtual, physical, executive, or combined node, blocking these from any other accesses and allowing only the embraced scenario to work with them (thus preventing possible competition for the node's assets that may lead to unexpected results). This resource blockage is automatically lifted after the embraced scenario terminates. If more than two scenarios are competing for the node's resources, they will be organized in a FIFO manner at the node.

exit—terminates the innermost loop in which it is included.

- **Grasping rules**

The rule's identifier can be expressed not only as a directly given name, but also by the result produced by a scenario of any complexity and treated as the rule's name. It can also be a compound one, integrated from multiple names provided by different scenarios, so in general we may have the following:

rule → *grasp* → *constant* | *variable* | *rule*({*grasp*,})

Under this extended definition, resulting from recursive SGL syntax, additional parameters can also associate with the rule's names, before embracing the main scenario operands. Such aggregation can simplify the structure of SGL scenarios, also making them more flexible and adjustable to changing goals and environments in which they operate.

3.5 Summary of Full SGL Syntax

Syntactic categories are shown next in italics, vertical bars separate alternatives, parts in braces indicate zero or more repetitions with a delimiter at the right, and constructs in brackets are optional. The remaining characters and words are the language symbols (including boldfaced braces).

grasp	→	*constant*	*variable*	[*rule*] [({*grasp*,})]
constant	→	*information*	*matter*	*special*	*custom*	*grasp*
information	→	*string*	*scenario*	*number*
string	→	'{*character*}'
scenario	→	{{*character*}}
number	→	[*sign*]{*digit*}[.{*digit*}[e[*sign*]{*digit*}]]
matter	→	"{*character*}"
special	→	thru	done	fail	fatal	infinite	nil	any	all	other	allother	current	passed	existing	neighbors	direct	forward	backward	synchronous	asynchronous	virtual	physical	executive	engaged	vacant	firstcome	unique
variable	→	*global*	*heritable*	*frontal*	*nodal*	*environmental*

global	→	G{*alphameric*}
heritable	→	H{*alphameric*}
frontal	→	F{*alphameric*}
nodal	→	N{*alphameric*}
environmental	→	TYPE | NAME | CONTENT | ADDRESS | QUALITIES | WHERE | BACK | PREVIOUS | PREDECESSOR | DOER | RESOURCES | LINK | DIRECTION | WHEN | TIME | STATE | VALUE | IDENTITY | IN | OUT | STATUS
rule	→	*type | usage | movement | creation | echoing | verification | assignment | advancement | branching | transference | exchange | timing | qualifying |* grasp
type	→	global | heritable | frontal | nodal | environmental | matter | number | string | scenario | constant | custom
usage	→	address | coordinate | content | index | time | speed | name | place | center | range | doer | node | link | unit
movement	→	hop | hopfirst | hopforth | move | shift | follow
creation	→	create | linkup | delete | unlink
echoing	→	state | rake | order | unit | unique | sum | count | first | last | min | max | random | average | sortup | sortdown | reverse | element | position | fromto | add | subtract | multiply | divide | degree | separate | unite | attach | append | common | withdraw | increment | decrement | access | invert | apply | location | distance

verification	→	equal | nonequal | less | lessorequal | more | moreorequal | bigger | smaller | heavier | lighter | longer | shorter | empty | nonempty | belong | notbelong | intersect | notintersect | yes | no
assignment	→	assign | assignpeers
advancement	→	advance | slide | repeat | align | fringe
branching	→	branch | sequence | parallel | if | or | and | orsequence | orparallel | andsequence | andparallel | choose | quickest | cycle | loop | sling | whirl | split | replicate
transference	→	run | call
exchange	→	input | output | send | receive | emit | get
timing	→	sleep | allowed
qualification	→	contain | release | trackless | free | blind | quit | abort | stay | lift | seize | exit

3.6 Conclusions

Full details on SGL, which continue an explanation of the language features started in Chapter 2, have been given. Different types of SGL constants, variables, and rules were presented with their syntax, semantics, and explanation of use. Summary of the full SGL syntax has been provided as well.

References

1. P. S. Sapaty, A Distributed Processing System, European Patent N 0389655, Publ. 10.11.93. European Patent Office.
2. P. S. Sapaty, Mobile Processing in Distributed and Open Environments. New York: John Wiley & Sons, 1999.

3. P. S. Sapaty, Ruling Distributed Dynamic Worlds. New York: John Wiley & Sons, 2005.
4. P. S. Sapaty, Managing Distributed Dynamic Systems with Spatial Grasp Technology. Springer, 2017.
5. P. S. Sapaty, Holistic Analysis and Management of Distributed Social Systems. Springer, 2018.
6. P. S. Sapaty, Complexity in International Security: A Holistic Spatial Approach. Emerald Publishing, 2019.
7. P. S. Sapaty, Symbiosis of Real and Simulated Worlds under Spatial Grasp Technology. Springer, 2021.
8. P. S. Sapaty, Spatial Grasp as a Model for Space-based Control and Management Systems. CRC Press, 2022.
9. P. S. Sapaty, The Spatial Grasp Model: Applications and Investigations of Distributed Dynamic Worlds. Emerald Publishing, 2023.
10. P. S. Sapaty, Managing Distributed Systems with Spatial Grasp Patterns, Mathematical Machines and Systems, 2023, 4.
11. P. S. Sapaty, Spatial Grasp Language (SGL), Advances in Image and Video Processing, 2016, 4(1). https://journals.scholarpublishing.org/index.php/AIVP/article/view/1922/1052
12. P. S. Sapaty, A Brief Introduction to the Spatial Grasp Language (SGL), Journal of Computer Science & Systems Biology, 2016, 9(2). www.omicsonline.org/computer-science-systems-biology.php
13. P. S. Sapaty, Spatial Grasp Language (SGL) for Distributed Management and Control, Journal of Robotics, Networking and Artificial Life, 2016, 3(2).
14. P. S. Sapaty, A Brief Introduction to the Spatial Grasp Language (SGL), Journal of Computer Science & Systems Biology, 2015, 9(2). www.researchgate.net/publication/307744279_A_Brief_Introduction_to_the_Spatial_Grasp_Language_SGL
15. P. S. Sapaty, The Language to Manage Distributed Robotized Systems. Proceedings of the Simulation Conference MODS, Zhukin, June 2007.
16. P. S. Sapaty, Wave-WP (World Processing) Technology and Applications. Proceedings of the International Conference & Exhibition Defence Technology Asia (Unmanned Vehicle Technology 2006, Mine & Warfare Surveillance Section), Singapore, 24–25 May 2006.
17. P. S. Sapaty, WAVE-WP (World Processing) Technology, Mathematical Machines and Systems, 2004, 3, 3–17.
18. P. S. Sapaty, Spatial Programming of Distributed Dynamic Worlds in WAVE. Presentation at the Special Colloquium "Internet Challenges", Hasso-Plattner-Institute, University of Potsdam, Berlin, 4 October 2002, 50 p.
19. P. S. Sapaty, Cooperative Exploration of Distributed Worlds in WAVE, International Journal of Artificial Life and Robotics, 2000, 4, 109–118.
20. P. S. Sapaty, High-Level Spatial Scenarios in WAVE. Proceedings of the 5th International Symposium AROB, Oita, January 2000, pp. 301–304.

21. P. S. Sapaty, Cooperative Conquest of Distributed Worlds in WAVE, Proceedings of the Symposium and Exhibition of the Unmanned Systems of the New Millennium, AUVSI'99, Baltimore, MD, 13–15 July 1999, 16 p.

22. P. S. Sapaty, Mobile Programming in WAVE, Mathematical Machines and Systems, 1998, 1, 3–31.

23. P. S. Sapaty, Live Demonstration of the WAVE System and Applications at the Workshop on Mobile Agents and Security 97, Maryland Center for Telecommunications Research, Department of Computer Science and Electrical Engineering, UMBC, 27–28 October 1997.

24. P. S. Sapaty, WAVE: Creating Dynamic Worlds Based on Mobile Cooperative Agents. Dartmouth Workshop on Transportable Agents, Dartmouth College, Hanover, NH, September 1996.

25. P. S. Sapaty, Mobile Wave Technology for Distributed Knowledge Processing in Open Networks. Proceedings of Workshop on New Paradigms in Information Visualization and Manipulation, in Conjunction with the Fourth International Conference on Information and Knowledge Management (CIKM'95), Baltimore, MD, December 1995.

26. P. S. Sapaty, A Brief Introduction to the WAVE Language, Report No. 3/93, Faculty of Informatics, University of Karlsruhe, 1993.

27. P. S. Sapaty, The WAVE Paradigm, Report No. 17/92, Faculty of Informatics, University of Karlsruhe, 1992.

28. P. S. Sapaty, The WAVE Paradigm, Proceedings of the JICSLP'92 Post-Conference Joint Workshop on Distributed and Parallel Implementations of Logic Programming Systems, Washington, DC, 13–14 November 1992.

29. P. S. Sapaty, The WAVE Model for Advanced Knowledge Processing. In Ambler, A. P., Agrawal, P., Moore, W. R. (Eds.), CAD Accelerators. Elsevier Science, 1990.

30. P. S. Sapaty, The WAVE Machine Project. Proceedings of the IFIP Workshop on Silicon Architectures for Neural Nets, St. Paul de Vence, 28–30 November 1990.

31. P. S. Sapaty, The WAVE Model for Advanced Knowledge Processing, Report No. OUEL 1803/89. Oxford: University of Oxford, 1989.

32. P. S. Sapaty, The WAVE-1: A New Ideology and Language of Distributed Processing on Graphs and Networks, Computers and Artificial Intelligence, 1987, 5.

33. P. S. Sapaty, The WAVE-0 Language as a Framework of Navigational Structures for Knowledge Bases Using Semantic Networks, Proceedings of USSR Academy of Sciences: Technical Cybernetics, 1986, 5.

34. P. S. Sapaty, A Wave Language for Parallel Processing of Semantic Networks, Computing and Artificial Intelligence, 1986, 5(4), 289–314.

35. P. S. Sapaty, The Wave Approach to Distributed Processing of Graphs and Networks. Proceedings of the International Working Conference on Knowledge and Vision Processing Systems, Smolenice, November 1986.

36. P. S. Sapaty, A Wave Approach to the Languages for Semantic Networks Processing. Proceedings of the International Workshop on Knowledge Representation. Kiev: Section 1: Artificial Intelligence, 1984.
37. P. S. Sapaty, On Possibilities of the Organization of a Direct Intercomputer Dialogue in ANALYTIC and FORTRAN Languages (Publ. No. 74–29). Kiev: Institute of Cybernetics Press, 1974.

4

DISTRIBUTED SYSTEM INTEGRITY UNDER SPATIAL GRASP TECHNOLOGY

4.1 Introduction

The aim of this chapter is to investigate the applicability and efficiency of the Spatial Grasp Model and Technology, which was developed and tested on numerous applications, for organizing and supporting the integrity of large distributed systems, which may cover any physical and virtual spaces. The rest of the chapter is organized as follows. Section 4.2 reviews a number of existing works on integrity, security, and recovery of distributed systems, grouped as integrity and recovery in distributed systems; recovery, security, and self-recovery in distributed systems; self-repair in distributed systems; and self-healing in autonomous systems. Section 4.3 reviews the main ideas of the Spatial Grasp Model and Technology (SGT) and its Spatial Grasp Language, described in Chapters 2 and 3. Section 4.4 shows how to use SGL for distributed system topology representation and creation, taking into account physical or virtual node coordinates, including full topology creation starting from all nodes in parallel and from a single node using a self-evolving topology spanning tree. Section 4.5 describes how to copy the already existing or newly created system topology, also in two cases, with the first one starting from all nodes in parallel and the second from a single node in a spanning tree mode. Section 4.6 shows how to create in SGL fully self-healing distributed topologies, which can self-reconstruct after simultaneous failures of any nodes, if at least a single node remains alive, thus providing a fully universal solution for system immortality, which can be effectively used for numerous applications, from IT to industry to security to defense. Section 4.7 concludes the chapter with the belief that SGT can provide the highest possible integrity of distributed dynamic systems unachievable by other models and technologies usually based on communicating parts or agents. References cite the analyzed publications on system integrity, as well as the books and latest papers on SGT.

4.2 Existing Approaches to Integrity, Security, and Recovery of Distributed Systems

The analyzed approaches, using mostly graph models for system representations and analysis, can be grouped by the following symbolic categories.

* **Integrity and recovery in distributed systems**

  Testing data integrity in distributed systems is considered in [1]. Security threats in a distributed environment are among the greatest threats in IT. A network provides the access path for both internal and external attacks, which makes it the key access point for any type of security threat. Securing a distributed infrastructure is not an easy task; it requires careful configuration and is subject to human errors. This paper presents a technique to test distributed environments against attacks on data integrity.

  Integrity of distributed control systems is discussed in [2], which focuses on the integrity of the overall distributed control system. It classifies properties that enable verification and proof of the integrity of different subsystems. Using this classification, it shows how to protect the overall system's integrity at different system levels. Based on an exemplary system in the domain of hydroelectric power plants, the paper shows practical examples of how to apply the results in the real world.

  Data integrity and recovery management in cloud computing is analyzed in [3]. A new methodology is proposed for data recovery and data management to assure high-level scalability and reliability of fault recognition and fault tolerance. The offered methodology allows for segmenting data and generating tokens for the data split-up, where a missing segment of any faulty node can be recovered from neighboring nodes.

- **Recovery, security, and self-recovery in distributed systems**

Recovery and security in a distributed system are considered in [4]. Distributed systems have immense practical value in the computerized world and have many applications, including scientific, engineering, commercial, and industrial. However, by their very nature of interconnectedness, distributed systems are subject to security issues and failures. These issues must be adequately addressed through effective techniques and methods to correct these problems.

A novel *two-stage sequential disaster recovery strategy for resilient cyber-physical distribution power systems* [5] is proposed with consideration of cyber-physical collaborative optimization. In the first stage, a mixed-integer linear programming model is formulated based on the integration of a transportation network, a cyber network, and a physical network. In the second stage, resources are rescheduled to repair the remaining damaged components.

Self-recovery of a distributed system after a large disruption is analyzed in [6]. Recovery of the systems hit by calamities, self-repairing of materials and tissues hit by radiation, and how the structures have to be designed are discussed. A group of animals such as rabbits and squirrels was created where the rabbits and squirrels could take control over territory by grouping into clusters. Then a large disruption scared all the animals and they started to scatter in every direction possible, with the next stage analyzing recovery depending on agent features.

- **Self-repair in distributed systems**

An approach for *self-repair in a distributed system using immunity-based diagnostic mobile agents* is offered in [7]. Self-repair has attracted much attention for fault tolerance in distributed computer network systems. In this paper, some units try to self-repair, that is, replace their data with data received from other units. Three different repairing conditions are proposed. Simulations evaluate the effectiveness of such conditions changing the numbers of initial abnormal hosts.

Minimum self-repairing graphs are discussed in [8]. A graph is self-repairing if it is 2-connected, such that removal of any single vertex results in no increase in distance between any pair of remaining vertices of the graph. The paper completely characterizes the class of minimum self-repairing graphs, which have the fewest edges for a given number of vertices.

- **Self-healing in autonomous systems**

A distributed formal-based model for self-healing behaviors in autonomous systems is discussed in [9]. Self-healing is one of the main features that characterize autonomic computing systems. Failure detection, recovery strategies, and reliability are of paramount importance to ensure continuous operation and correct functioning even in the presence of a given maximum amount of faulty components. A distributed formal model is offered for specification, verification, and analysis of self-healing behaviors in autonomous systems.

Self-healing dilemmas in distributed systems with fault correction vs. fault tolerance are analyzed in [10]. Measuring, understanding, and resolving self-healing dilemmas is a timely challenge and a critical requirement given the rise of distributed ledgers, edge computing, and the Internet of Things in several energy, transport, and health applications. The paper contributes a novel and general-purpose modeling of fault scenarios during system runtime. Methods are proposed to improve self-healing of large-scale decentralized systems at the design phase.

Self-healing networks that take into account redundancy and structure are discussed in [11]. The paper introduces the concept of self-healing in the field of complex network modeling. In particular, self-healing capabilities are implemented through distributed communication protocols that exploit redundant links to recover the connectivity of the system. The paper then analyzes the effect of the level of redundancy on the resilience to multiple failures; in particular, it measures the fraction of nodes still served for increasing levels of network damages.

A decentralized self-healing approach for network topology maintenance is covered in [12]. The paper proposes a multi-agent solution for recovering networks from node failures.

To preserve the network topology, the proposed approach relies on local information about the network's structure, which is collected and disseminated at runtime. These results validate the viability of the proposed self-healing solution, offering two variant implementations with diverse performance characteristics.

4.3 Spatial Grasp Model and Technology Basics

This reviews only key ideas of the basic model and technology that may be useful to comprehend more quickly the material of this chapter, with technology details in Chapters 2 and 3; see also [13–30]. Within Spatial Grasp Model and Technology, a high-level operational scenario is represented as an active self-evolving pattern rather than a traditional program. This pattern expressed in recursive Spatial Grasp Language (SGL), starting at any world point (or points), propagates, replicates, modifies, covers, and matches the distributed environment in parallel wavelike mode. This propagation also combines feedback echoing of the reached control states and obtained data, which may be remote, for making higher-level decisions, altogether providing holistic solutions unachievable by other models and systems. SGL allows for expressing direct space presence and operations with unlimited parallelism. Its universal recursive organization with operational scenarios called *grasp* can be expressed just by a single string:

$$grasp \quad \rightarrow \quad constant \mid variable \mid rule \; (\{grasp,\})$$

The SGL *rule* expresses a certain action, control, description, or context accompanied with operands, which can themselves be any *grasp* too. Each SGL interpreter copy can handle and process multiple active SGL scenario code that freely evolves and propagates in space and between the interpreters.

4.4 Distributed System Topology Representation and Creation

A topology example in the form of a graph with named nodes and links, which is distributed in two-dimensional physical space, is shown in Figure 4.1.

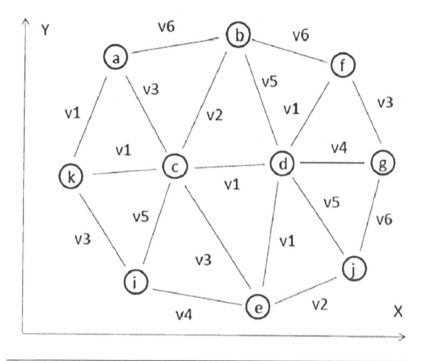

Figure 4.1   Representation of distributed systems topology in a physical-virtual graph mode.

- **Representing topology with node coordinates**

Compact textual representation of this topology assigned to variables Top (with node names followed by lists of named links leading to named neighbors) and Loc (having node names w followed by their Cw location coordinates expressed in some physical or virtual notation) may be as follows.

```
Top = (a: (v1:k, v3:c, v6:b), b: (v6:a, v2:c, v5:d, v6:f),
     f: (v6:b, v1:d, v3:g), k: (v1:a, v1:c, v3:i), c: (v1:k,
     v3:a, v2:b, v1::d, v3:e, v5:i),
d: (v1:c, v5:b, v1:f, v4:g, v5:j, v1:e), g: (v4:d, v3:f,
     v6:j),
i: (v3:k, v5:c, v4:e), e: (v4:I, v3:c, v1:d, v2:j),
j: (v2:e, v5:d, v6:g))
Loc = (a:Ca, b:Cb, c:Cc, d:Cd, e:Ce, f:Cf, g:Cg, I:Ci,
j:Cj, k:Ck)
```

- **Creating full topology—starting from all nodes in parallel**

Creating only single nodes (without connections to neighbors) in proper space locations (with known coordinates to be used by rule coord) can be done in parallel by the following SGL text, where operation split creates as many parallel braches as there are elements in the embraced variable Loc, with each element addressed by SGL environmental variable VAL (short for VALUE) in the corresponding branch:

```
split(Loc); create _ node(VAL[1], coord(VAL[2]))
```

Creating full topology in parallel (i.e. all nodes with named links to other nodes, also nodes having names and coordinates in virtual or physical space) can be done by the following scenario (resolving competition of neighboring nodes attempting to create the same link between them, allowing this for nodes having higher value of their name than of the neighbor) may be as follows; see also Figure 4.2:

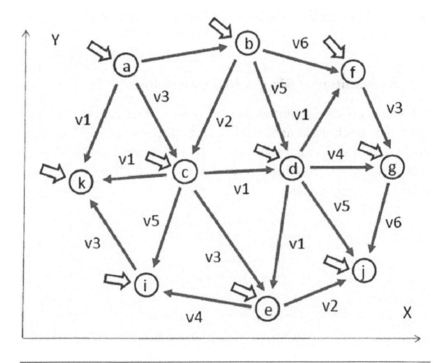

Figure 4.2 Creating distributed networked structure in parallel.

```
Top = . . .; frontal(Loc) = . . .;
align(split(Top); frontal(NN) = VAL[2];
      create _ node(VAL[1], coord(Loc:VAL[1]));
split(NN); NAME > VAL[2];
linkup(VAL[1], node(VAL[2], coord(Loc:VAL[2])))
```

In this scenario, the rule `split` is used twice, first creating as many parallel branches as there are network nodes, and then for each node forms its own parallel branches for dealing with all their neighbors).

- **Creating full topology—starting from a single node**

Creating the same topology but starting from a given node, using spatially evolving spanning tree mode, may be done by the following scenario (see also Figure 4.3):

```
Top = . . .; frontal(Loc) = . . .; Start = . . .;
create _ node(Start, coord(Loc:Start));
repeat(
  split(Top:NAME);
  or _ seq((empty(see(Loc:VAL[2]));
          create(link(VAL[1], node(VAL[2],
              coord(Loc:VAL[2])))),
          (NAME > VAL[2];
          linkup(VAL[1], node(VAL[2],
              coord(Loc:VAL[2]))); quit)))
```

As the network forming spanning tree process develops asynchronously in physical space, the competition between neighbors for creation of the same nodes is resolved by first testing whether the node's physical position is still empty, before its creation, otherwise just linking to the already existing node and quitting.

4.5 Copying System Topology

- **Copying full topology starting from all nodes in parallel**

Copying the already existing or just created full topology, starting from all its nodes in parallel, with obtaining its textual representation in already mentioned variables `Top` and `Loc`, can be done by

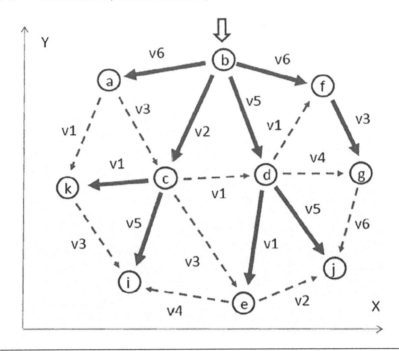

Figure 4.3 Creating distributed networked structure from a single node in a spanning tree mode.

the following (with the search Area defined, say, by 3D coordinates or any other descriptions, using zone addresses in virtual spaces too):

```
Area = (X1 _ X2, Y1 _ Y2, Z1 _ Z2);
Top = (hop _ nodes(Area, all);
        append(NAME, unit(hop _ links(all); LINK & NAME)));
Loc = (hop _ nodes(Area, all); NAME & WHERE)
```

For depicting the work of this scenario, Figure 4.2 can be used here too (except for the links' creation directions, which may differ).

• **Copying full topology starting from a single node**

This may be done in a self-evolving spanning tree mode, say, starting randomly from any single graph node, as follows:

```
Area = . . .; hopfirst _ node(Area, any);
Top = repeat(blind(append(NAME, unit(hop _ links(all);
            LINK & NAME))), hopfirst _ links(all));
hopfirst _ node(Area, any);
Loc = repeat(blind(NAME & WHERE), hopfirst _ links(all))
```

Figure 4.3 can be used for this scenario too (ignoring, however, the links' creation directions, which may differ here).

4.6 Fully Self-Healing Topologies

We can also easily write in SGL a full recovery scenario which, initially applied in all nodes, will allow the whole topology to self-recover after arbitrary damages (if even a single node still remains alive). Each node, seeing the absence of its neighbors and/or links to them, will provide their restoration, including supplying the restored nodes with the capability of doing the same for absent neighbors if such are noticed too, and so on. This makes the whole topology alive and self-healing, with damages even appearing any time and simultaneously in many nodes. Figure 4.4 and the following SGL scenario explain these unique self-healing capabilities, actually allowing for "immortality" of distributed system topologies under SGL and SGT.

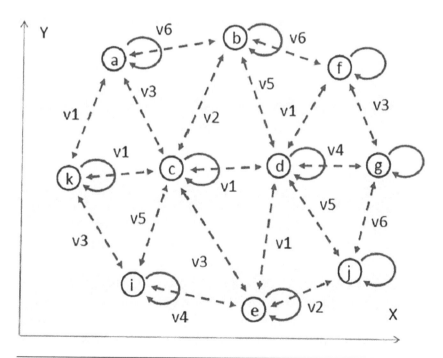

Figure 4.4   Making distributed networked systems constantly self-analyzing and self-repairing from any damages.

```
frontal(Top = . . ., Loc = . . ., Business = {. . .},
Recovery =
 {split(Top:NAME);
  repeat _ stay(
    sleep(delay);
    empty(see(Loc:VAL[2]));
    create(link(VAL[1], node(VAL[2],
          coord(Loc:VAL[2])));
    free(run(Business, Recovery)))});
Area = . . .; hop _ nodes(Area, all); run(Business, Recovery)
```

The prior scenario uses the universal recovering facility as a procedure assigns to variable `Recovery`, which with another, traditional, node business procedure in variable `Business` is always transferred to the just recovered nodes and activated there (both procedures being spatially transferable in `frontal` variables). For the prior scenario, any number of nodes can be killed at any time, also simultaneously, as in, for example, the following eight nodes:

```
Area = . . .; delete(hop _ nodes(Area, (a, b, c, d, g, i, e,
j)))
```

The full topology self-recovery after such damage will simultaneously originate from two still remaining nodes k and f, as shown in Figure 4.5, spreading afterwards to all other dynamically restored nodes, which in their turn, spread this further, if needed, and so on.

4.7 Conclusions

We have investigated the application of distributed Spatial Grasp Model and Technology for management of large distributed networked systems, from their expression, creation, copying, and modeling to continuous self-analysis and self-recovery from any damages. Based on compact recursive self-spreading, self-matching, and self-evolving operational code, SGT can provide the highest possible integrity of distributed dynamic systems unachievable by any other models and technologies, which are usually based on communicating parts or agents, with known difficulties of achieving the needed whole parameters and behavior. The super-virus mode of operation of the

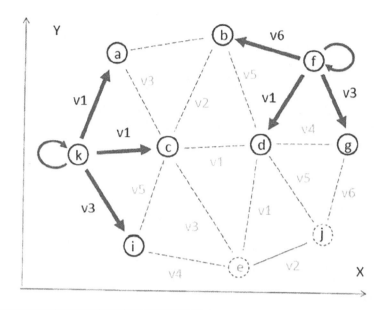

Figure 4.5   Distributed system full self-recovery starting from two still remaining nodes.

approach offered, where any holes and damages can be immediately self-repaired and covered by the recursive self-spreading active code, can make the large distributed dynamic systems actually "immortal" in many important applications. The latter may cover industry, finance, security, environment, defense, space conquest, and many other fields. The offered distributed control technology, by our experience with its previous versions in different countries, can be easily implemented on any existing platforms and integrated with other networked systems, forming altogether powerful spatial engines effectively operating in both terrestrial and celestial environments.

References

1. M. Mittal, R. Sangani, K. Srivastava, Testing Data Integrity in Distributed Systems, Procedia Computer Science, 2015, 45, 446–452. www.sciencedirect.com/science/article/pii/S1877050915003130

2. T. Rauter, Integrity of Distributed Control Systems. Student Forum of the 46th Annual IEEE/IFIP International Conference on Dependable Systems and Networks (hal-01318372), Toulouse, June 2016. https://hal. science/hal-01318372/file/DSN-Student-Forum_%237_Integrity-of-Distributed-Control-Systems.pdf

3. G. Sivanandham, J. M. Gnanasekar, Data Integrity and Recovery Management in Cloud Systems. Proceedings of the Fourth International Conference on Inventive Systems and Control (ICISC 2020) DVD Part Number: CFP20J06-DVD. www.researchgate.net/publication/343751352_Data_Integrity_and_Recovery_Management_in_Cloud_Systems

4. G. K. Sodhi, Recovery and Security in Distributed System, International Journal of Advanced Research in Computer and Communication Engineering, 2015, 4(12). www.ijarcce.com/upload/2015/december-15/IJARCCE%20105.pdf

5. X. Sun, J. Chen, H. Zhao, W. Zhang, Y. Zhang, Sequential Disaster Recovery Strategy for Resilient Distribution Network Based on Cyber–Physical Collaborative Optimization, IEEE Transactions on Smart Grid, 2023, 14(2), 1173–1187. https://doi.org/10.1109/TSG.2022.3198696. https://ieeexplore.ieee.org/document/9857641

6. V. Popa-Simil, H. Poston, Mrs. Thomas, L. Popa-Simil, Self-Recovery of a Distributed System After a Large Disruption, New Mexico Supercomputing Challenge, Final Report, 1 April 2012. www.supercomputingchallenge.org/11-12/finalreports/15.pdf

7. Y. Watanabe, S. Sato, Y. Ishida, An Approach for Self-repair in Distributed System Using Immunity-Based Diagnostic Mobile Agents. In Negoita, M. G. et al. (Eds.), KES 2004, LNAI 3214. Berlin and Heidelberg: Springer-Verlag, 2004, pp. 504–510. https://link.springer.com/chapter/10.1007/978-3-540-30133-2_66

8. A. M. Farley, A. Proskurowski, Minimum Self-Repairing Graphs, Graphs and Combinatorics, 1997, 13, 345–351. https://doi.org/10.1007/BF03353012. https://link.springer.com/article/10.1007/BF03353012

9. I. B. Hafaiedh, M. B. Slimane, A Distributed Formal-Based Model for Self-Healing Behaviors in Autonomous Systems: From Failure Detection to Self-Recovery, The Journal of Supercomputing, 2022, 78, 18725–18753. https://link.springer.com/article/10.1007/s11227-022-04614-0

10. J. Nikolic, N. Jubatyrov, E. Pournaras, Self-Healing Dilemmas in Distributed Systems: Fault Correction vs. Fault Tolerance, Journal of Latex Class Files, 2021, X(X). https://arxiv.org/pdf/2007.05261.pdf

11. W. Quattrociocchi, G. Caldarelli, A. Scala, Self-Healing Networks: Redundancy and Structure, PLoS One, 2014, 9(2), e87986. file:///C:/Users/user/Downloads/2014-02Self-healingnetworksredundancyandstructure.pdf

12. A. Rodríguez, J. Gómez, A. Diaconescu, A Decentralised Self-Healing Approach for Network Topology Maintenance, Autonomous Agents and Multi-Agent Systems, 2021, 35, Article Number 6. https://link.springer.com/article/10.1007/s10458-020-09486-3

13. P. S. Sapaty, A Distributed Processing System, European Patent N 0389655, Publ. 10.11.93. European Patent Office.

14. P. S. Sapaty, Mobile Processing in Distributed and Open Environments. New York: John Wiley & Sons, 1999.

15. P. S. Sapaty, Ruling Distributed Dynamic Worlds. New York: John Wiley & Sons, 2005.
16. P. S. Sapaty, Managing Distributed Dynamic Systems with Spatial Grasp Technology. Springer, 2017.
17. P. S. Sapaty, Holistic Analysis and Management of Distributed Social Systems. Springer, 2018.
18. P. S. Sapaty, Complexity in International Security: A Holistic Spatial Approach. Emerald Publishing, 2019.
19. P. S. Sapaty, Symbiosis of Real and Simulated Worlds under Spatial Grasp Technology. Springer, 2021.
20. P. S. Sapaty, Spatial Grasp as a Model for Space-based Control and Management Systems. CRC Press, 2022.
21. P. S. Sapaty, The Spatial Grasp Model: Applications and Investigations of Distributed Dynamic Worlds. Emerald Publishing, 2023.
22. P. S. Sapaty, Distributed Control Technology for Air and Missile Defence Operations, International Relations and Diplomacy, 2022, 10(4), 141–157. https://doi.org/10.17265/2328-2134/2022.04.001. www.davidpublisher.com/Public/uploads/Contribute/6364741a7b432.pdf
23. P. S. Sapaty, Relation of Spatial Grasp Paradigm to Higher Psychological and Mental Concepts, Acta Scientific Computer Sciences, 2022, 4(12). https://actascientific.com/ASCS/pdf/ASCS-04-0359.pdf
24. P. S. Sapaty, Seeing and Managing Distributed Worlds with Spatial Grasp Paradigm, Acta Scientific Computer Sciences, 2022, 4(12). https://actascientific.com/ASCS/pdf/ASCS-04-0365.pdf
25. P. S. Sapaty, Comprehending Distributed Worlds with the Spatial Grasp Paradigm, Mathematical Machines and Systems, 2022, 1. www.immsp.kiev.ua/publications/articles/2022/2022_1/01_22_Sapaty.pdf
26. P. S. Sapaty, Spatial Management of Air and Missile Defence Operations, Mathematical Machines and Systems, 2023, 1. www.immsp.kiev.ua/publications/articles/2023/2023_1/01_23_Sapaty.pdf
27. P. S. Sapaty, Providing Distributed System Integrity under Spatial Grasp Technology, Mathematical Machines and Systems, 2023, 2. www.immsp.kiev.ua/publications/articles/2023/2023_2/02_23_Sapaty.pdf
28. P. S. Sapaty, Providing Global Awareness in Distributed Dynamic Systems, International Relations and Diplomacy, 2023, 11(2), 87–100. https://doi.org/10.17265/2328-2134/2023.02.002. www.davidpublisher.com/Public/uploads/Contribute/6486c3d05a6cc.pdf
29. P. S. Sapaty, Simulating Distributed Consciousness with Spatial Grasp Model, Mathematical Machines and Systems, 2023, 3.
30. P. S. Sapaty, Managing Distributed Systems with Spatial Grasp Patterns, Mathematical Machines and Systems, 2023, 4.

5

Providing Global Awareness in Distributed Dynamic Systems

5.1 Introduction

Awareness, especially its global capabilities, is extremely important in our everyday life. In the most general terms, global awareness is considered a capacity that incorporates the attitudes, knowledge, and skills necessary to navigate the challenges and opportunities of a globalized world. It provides understanding of values and beliefs of different cultures, analyzes solutions to international problems, and makes recommendations that contribute to the global common good. This chapter investigates the application of Spatial Grasp Technology for solving diverse problems in large distributed dynamic systems that can provide, from any inside or outside point, sufficient awareness of their coverage, structures, and functionalities. The rest of the chapter is organized as follows. Section 5.2 provides a review of the meaning of awareness and existing approaches for its expression and support, which include distributed and situation awareness, its practical, theoretic, and technological issues, and awareness and control of real systems and networks. Emphasizing the complexity of real distributed systems, it stresses the necessity of new management approaches with high system awareness. Section 5.3 reviews the main ideas of the Spatial Grasp Model and Technology (SGT) and its Spatial Grasp Language, described in Chapters 2 and 3. Section 5.4 provides an example of a hypothetical distributed system with 100 different nodes interlinked by various relations, with nodes and links having physical and virtual properties, which is analyzed in detail in the following sections. Elementary awareness queries are considered in Section 5.5 and include the names of all global communication nodes, all working nodes, combined communication-working nodes, top management

 DOI: 10.1201/9781003425267-5

nodes, and nodes with links to other businesses. Finding paths in the whole network is covered in Section 5.6, including a single path from start to end nodes, also with using only certain link types, shortest path tree (SPT) from start to all other nodes, and finding shortest paths from start to end nodes on the basis of SPT created. Section 5.7 considers finding some peculiar structures in the system network that may reflect its diversity and complexity. These include all articulation points in the communication network, discovery and exhibition of all maximum cliques inside working collectives, and maximum cliques in the communication network. Section 5.8 provides some higher-level knowledge about the distributed system, which includes evaluating the total length of a global communication network, listing all working collectives, determining which collective has the maximum number of offices, outlining X_Y area occupied by the whole distributed system, also inferring business cooperation network between different organizations as a whole. Section 5.9 concludes the chapter with the hope that any imaginable and even so far unimaginable awareness queries and solutions in distributed systems can be obtained by recursive scenarios in SGL. References provide review on the existing publications on awareness and the chosen investigative technology.

5.2 Awareness and Its Existing Approaches

This section provides a review of the meaning of awareness and its different options and also analyzes existing approaches for its expression and support.

- **Awareness definitions**

  Awareness [1] is a concept about knowing, perceiving, and being cognizant of events. The concept is often synonymous to consciousness and is also understood as being consciousness itself. The states of awareness are also associated with the states of experience so that the structure represented in awareness is mirrored in the structure of experience.

  In spatial awareness [2] the definition of visual-spatial relations is the ability to visually perceive two or more objects in relation to each other and yourself. Spatial reasoning is how we understand how things (including ourselves) move and interact in relation to the physical space around them. It also involves understanding the relationships of objects as they change position.

Total Information Awareness [3] was a mass detection program by the United States Information Awareness Office. It operated under this title from February to May 2003 before being renamed Terrorism Information Awareness.

• **Distributed situation awareness**

Distributed computing [4] is defined as a system consisting of software components spread over different computers but running as a single entity. A distributed system can be an arrangement of different configurations, such as mainframes, computers, workstations, and minicomputers. Distributed systems are the most significant foundation of modern computing systems due to their capability of providing scalable and improved performance.

Distributed situation awareness [5] is focused on situation awareness in domains such as defense, transport, and process control. A significant contribution has been to initiate a shift from considering individual human operator situation awareness to considering the situation awareness of human and nonhuman teams, organizations, and even sociotechnical systems. The distributed situation awareness model has become increasingly relevant for modern-day systems and problems.

Contemporary thinking on distributed situation awareness (DSA) [6] has developed over the past decade from a concept into a testable theory with associated methodology. Early forays into understanding the nature of DSA are presented together with examples of case applications, where DSA is based on the original ideas from distributed cognition.

• **Practical and theoretic issues on distributed situation awareness**

Seven issues on distributed situation awareness measurement [7] consider situation awareness (SA) as an emergent property of a complex sociotechnical system rather than an individual endeavor. This work collects some of the most crucial issues surrounding the existing SA measurements techniques that arose under the complex sociotechnical systems settings, moving beyond the existing network-based approaches.

Real-world awareness in distributed organizations [8] marks the state of being informed incorporated with an understanding of project-related activities, states, or relationships of each individual employee within a given group as a whole. Awareness becomes a concurrent process that amplifies the exigency of easy routes for staff to be able to access this information, deferred or decentralized, in a formalized and problem-oriented way.

In distributed situation awareness theory, measurement and application [9] situation awareness is the term that is used within human factors circles to describe the level of awareness that operators have of the situation. It focuses on how operators develop and maintain a sufficient understanding of what is going on in order to achieve success in task performance. This construct has become a fundamental theme in system design and evaluation and has received considerable attention from the research community.

- **Technological issues of distributed awareness**

Distributed situation awareness is becoming a "middleware" between the new economic sociology and embedded open innovation [10]. Modern societies are comprised of open systems whose internal elements interact with their environment. These diverse elements are integrated in multi-agent sociotechnical systems exhibiting an open process of information fusion. A combination of distributed situation awareness and embedded open innovation can contribute to change our view of collaboration, develop a holistic and systemic culture, along with models based on the sociotechnical perspective.

Context awareness in distributed computing systems is considered in [11]. Creating robust systems that deal with and consist of both the physical world and networked computing nodes is relevant to a large class of applications. Due to the importance of such cyber-physical systems to our everyday lives and economies, it is important to investigate and develop new methodologies for programming such systems. Context information in the computation may be part of the answer to dealing with the emergent behavior and dynamicity of cyber-physical systems.

- **Distributed situational awareness and control of real systems and networks**

Distributed situational awareness in robot swarms is considered in [12]. Many-robot systems are becoming a reality for large companies that can invest in bespoke solutions. These systems often require carefully engineered infrastructure and a central planner to coordinate the robots. Distributed situational awareness allows swarms of low-cost robots to rapidly and accurately capture the state of an environment and act accordingly, with no central data storage, modeling, or control.

Distributed situational awareness and control are discussed in [13], which describes the benefits of applying distributed unmanned aerial vehicle (UAV) teams to situational awareness problems. The situational awareness problem is divided into two components: decentralized data fusion and team decision-making to maximize information gain. The work outlines the mathematical formulation of the general team decision-making problem and how to yield tractable, online solutions.

A review of network situation awareness for operation and maintenance is provided in [14]. In order to meet the requirements of high-tech enterprises for high power quality, high-quality operation and maintenance in smart distribution networks (SDN) is becoming increasingly important, and situation awareness begins to gain the significant interest of scholars and managers, especially after the integration of renewable energy into SDN. The paper divides SA into three stages: detection, comprehension, and projection.

An overview of reinforcement learning algorithms for handover management in ultra-dense small cell networks, which may be used for distributed awareness, is considered in [15]. The fifth generation (5G) wireless technology emerged with marvelous effort in design, deployment, and standardization of the upcoming wireless network generation. Artificial intelligence and machine learning techniques are well capable of supporting the latest 5G technologies that are expected to deliver high data rate to massive machine type communications.

- **Complexity of distributed systems with new management approaches needed**

This brief review confirms the enormous complexity of real distributed dynamic systems and how to deal with them properly. Such systems need for their observation, understanding, management, and control the most advanced theoretical and practical approaches, mechanisms, and technologies that provide local and global awareness of their structures and organizations, which may be needed to be available from any of their points, and to which this paper is devoted.

5.3 Spatial Grasp Model and Technology Basics

This section reviews only the key ideas of the basic model and technology, which may be useful for comprehending more quickly the material of this chapter, with technology details in Chapters 2 and 3 and more in [16–33]. Within Spatial Grasp Model and Technology, a high-level operational scenario is represented as an active self-evolving pattern rather than a traditional program. This pattern expressed in recursive Spatial Grasp Language (SGL), starting at any world point (or points), propagates, replicates, modifies, covers, and matches the distributed environment in parallel wavelike mode. This propagation also combines feedback echoing of the reached control states and obtained data, which may be remote, for making higher-level decisions, altogether providing holistic solutions unachievable by other models and systems. The SGL allows for expressing direct space presence and operations with unlimited parallelism. Its universal recursive organization with operational scenarios called *grasp* can be expressed just by a single string:

$$grasp \quad \rightarrow \quad constant \mid variable \mid rule \; (\{grasp,\})$$

The SGL *rule* expresses certain action, control, description, or context accompanied with operands, which can themselves be any *grasp* too.

Each SGL interpreter copy can handle and process multiple active SGL scenario code that is freely evolving and propagating in space and between the interpreters.

5.4 Hypothetical Distributed System Example

In order to analyze and show practical SGT and SGL capabilities for providing local and global awareness of any distributed systems, we will be using their formal (also rather hypothetical) representation as a large heterogeneous distributed network (of exactly 100 nodes), with different kinds of nodes having both names and physical coordinates, which are interconnected by different types of links, as in Figure 5.1 and Figure 5.2.

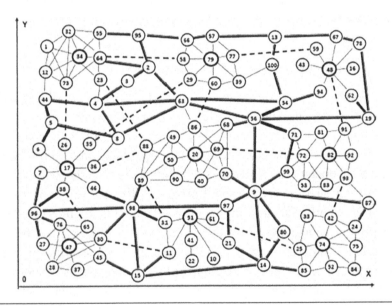

Figure 5.1   Hypothetical networked image of a large distributed heterogeneous system.

gc	wr
Global communications	Work relations
ibl	bc
Inter-business links	Business cooperation

Figure 5.2   Different types of network internode links.

This system example reflects different working organizations as collectives (having hardened top management nodes), which may have hierarchical or more complex organizations, with working relations (wr) between nodes-departments. These organizations are interconnected by a global communication (gc) network (having gc links) which may reflect power and resources supplies and exchanges, electronic links, physical road connections, and so on. This global communication network has its own communication nodes (with only gc links) to keep global coverage, while some of its nodes are common with working nodes (these have both wr and gc links) via which different organizations are supplied with global system communication and transportation resources. Different organizations may also have a peculiar cooperation (with inter-business links, or ibl) between their special departments (which, say, may reflect additional phone or internet connections, or just personal friendship and interests). By these local links the organizations may be generally considered as having global cooperation with each other (it will be shown later how these business cooperation, or bc, links can be inferred between the whole organizations).

In the following sections we will be showing practical solutions in SGL of useful system observation tasks (actually any imaginable and perhaps as yet unimaginable) that provide awareness about different points, parts, and the whole of the system of Figure 5.1, which may be detailed, summarized, or generalized. And the request for such knowledge can be issued at any time and from any points inside or outside the system and returned to the same or other points, thus providing global and mutual awareness of its contents, structures, and organizations for everybody and any institution.

5.5 Elementary Awareness Queries

These requests provide the most general knowledge about the network components.

- **Listing names of all global communication nodes**

```
output(hop _ nodes(all); TYPE = global; NAME) or
output(hop _ nodes(all); true(hop _ links(gc)); NAME)
```

Result: (55, 95, 66, 37, . . . , 9, 14, 85)—about half of all nodes, which may include some working nodes with double functionality.

- **Listing all working nodes (top managers including)**

```
output(hop_nodes(all); true(hop_links(wr)); NAME)
```

Result: (1, 32, 55, . . . , 85, 52, 24)—almost half of all nodes too. These may also include some global communication nodes with double functionality.

- **Naming combined communication-working nodes**

```
output(hop_nodes(all); true(and(hop_links(wr),
hop_links(gc))); NAME)
```

Result: (55, 64, 44, 4, 66, 57, 100, 67, 78, 94, 62, 6, 7, 8, 38, 46, 89, 68, 70, 71, 99, 19, 87, 27, 76, 30, 31, 11, 97, 21, 80, 24, 85)

- **Naming all top management nodes**

```
output(hop_nodes(all); TYPE = top; NAME)
```

Result: (34, 79, 48, 17, 20, 82, 47, 51, 74)

- **Listing nodes with links to other businesses (which may include working, top management, and combined working-communicating nodes)**

```
output(hop_nodes(all); true(hop_links(ibl)); NAME)
```

Result: (64, 58, 77, 59, 35, 29, 36, 23, 88, 69, 72, 38, 65, 30, 11, 61, 25, 42, 93, 48, 91)

5.6 Discovering Different Paths between Nodes in the System Networks

- **Finding any single path (i.e. without node repetitions) from Start to End nodes**

```
nodal(Start = . . .); frontal(End = . . ., Path);
output(hop_first(Start); Path = NAME;
       repeat(hop_first_links(all); Path &= NAME;
              if(NAME == End, terminate_blind(Path))))
```

If, for example, Start = 23, End = 72, the path found may be (23, 88, 50, 20, 69, 72), with accidentally used links ibl and wr.

- **Finding any single path (without repetitions) from Start to End nodes using only certain link types**

```
nodal(Start = 23); frontal(End = 72, Links = (wr, gc),
Path);
output(hop _ first(Start); Path = NAME;
        repeat(hop _ first _ links(Links); Path &= NAME;
                if(NAME == End, terminate _ blind(Path))))
```

If only wr and gc links are allowed with the same Start and End nodes, as previously, the path found may be (23, 4, 63, 56, 71, 72).

- **Shortest path tree (SPT) from Start node to all other nodes (assuming all links with length 1)**

```
nodal(Start = . . ., Parent, Distance); frontal(Length);
hop _ node(Start); Distance = 0;
repeat(hop _ links(all); increment(Length, 1);
        or(Distance == nil, Distance > Length);
        Distance = Length; Parent = PREVIOUS)
```

This SPT covering all network nodes, beginning from Start, will be recorded in the network structure rather than output, where in each node reference to its prior tree node is fixed in the nodal variable Parent.

- **Shortest path tree (SPT) from Start node to all other nodes with taking into account physical distances between nodes**

For this, we should change incrementing Length in the previous scenario (which can result in a different SPT) to `increment(Length, far(BERORE, WHERE))`

- **Finding shortest path (SP) from Start to Final nodes on the basis of SPT found**

a. *Starting in the final node and issuing the path in the starting node.* The following scenario for the path from Start to Final originates in the final node and then moves up the SPT while collecting the passed path in a reverse order (using data on predecessor nodes recorded in variable Parent), until reaching Start node, issuing it from there.

```
nodal(Final = . . .); frontal(Path, Start);
hop _ node(Final);
output(repeat(Path = NAME && Path; hop(Parent);
              if(NAME == Start, quit(Path))))
```

b. *Beginning from Start, moving downward the tree, and issuing the collected path in Start.* This will accumulate all possible paths down the SPT, which may grow in parallel, while terminating the correct branch reaching Final and echoing the collected Path from there to Start. The advantage of this solution over the previous one is that the needed path was found by initially accessing only the Start node, whereas in the previous solutions we had to start it from Final, and for this had to know its location in advance. But the previous solution was much more economic, as for the current one we had to grow a number of paths via the SPT, and only one of them appeared to be correct.

```
nodal(Start = . . .); frontal(Final = . . ., Path);
hop _ node(Start);
output(repeat(Path = append(Path, NAME);
              if(NAME == Final, terminate(Path));
              hop _ links(all); Parent == PREVIOUS))
```

With Start = 60 and End = 28, such a path may be (60, 86, 49, 89, 98, 30, 28).

5.7 Finding Peculiar Structures

Different parts of the system in Figure 5.1 may have different, often complex, networking structures that may reflect their purpose, functionality, and general capabilities. Among these, articulation points (reflecting the network's weakest points) and cliques (as the most powerful structures) may be of particular interest and importance.

- **Finding articulation points (AP)**

These are the network nodes that when deleted split the network into disconnected parts. The following scenario will find all AP in parallel in the communications network with gc type of links.

```
hop _ nodes(all); true(hop _ links(gc)); COLOR = NAME;
hop _ first(stay);
output(
   and _ seq((hop _ first _ link(any, gc);
              repeat(hop _ first _ links(all, gc))),
             hop _ first _ links(all, gc),
           done(NAME)))
```

Result: (56, 9, 87, 14, 98, 96, 5, 15, 19, 95, 2, 87)

This scenario, starting in all gc-connected nodes, first goes by any single gc link to a neighboring node and marks the whole part of the network starting from it with a special COLOR (the starting node included). After this, it tries to move via all other gc links from the same starting node to see if at least a single unmarked node is reached. That will indicate that this starting node separates the whole network into disconnected parts, and its name will be printed together with other such nodes.

- **Finding maximum cliques (MC) inside all working collectives**

Cliques are the strongest network parts represented as full graphs with any node connected to any other one. The following scenario finds all maximum cliques in the networks of working collectives, with the number of their nodes equal or higher to the given Threshold (chosen to be four for obtaining more interesting cases).

```
output(
   hop _ first _ nodes(all, TYPE = top);
   fringe(repeat(done(stay), hop _ first _ links(wr)));
   contain(
     frontal(Clique = NAME, Threshold = 4);
     repeat(
       or _ seq((hop _ links(all, wr); notbelong(NAME,
```

```
Clique);
true(and _ parallel(hop(link _ any(wr),
nodes _ all(Clique))));
if(PREDECESSOR > NAME, append(Clique, NAME),
abort)), (count(Clique) >= Threshold;
done _ unit(Clique))))))
```

Starting from all working nodes (accessed from top managers), it spreads via links to other working nodes and adds each new node to the frontal variable Clique if this node has connection with all previous clique nodes, until this becomes possible, then outputs the obtained clique in Clique. To avoid duplicates, which can appear because any clique can form independently from all its nodes, the clique formation should only be continued in a unique order by comparing the value of new node in NAME with the value of previous node in environmental variable PREDECESSOR (using for comparison just node names), immediately terminating otherwise.

The resultant cliques will be as follows: (73, 34, 32, 12, 1), (76, 47, 28, 27), (86, 69, 68, 20), (70, 69, 40, 20), (83, 82, 72, 53), (75, 74, 42, 24); see also their graphical images in Figure 5.3.

To show the possible cliques in particular working collectives, not all as earlier, we should start only from their top management nodes (shown as heavier ones in Figure 5.1 and Figure 5.3), where, say, the collective with top manager 20 has two cliques (86, 69, 68, 20) and (70, 69, 40, 20), while others have only one or none.

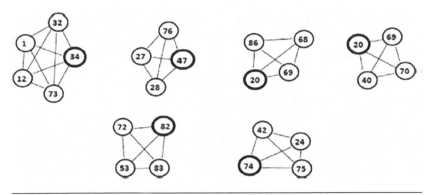

Figure 5.3 Resultant maximum cliques in the working collectives.

- **Finding MC in the whole communication network**

To do this, we should change the following parameters in the prior scenario, as follows, including a lower Threshold as communication networks have a less complex structure; see also Figure 5.1:

```
TYPE = global, Threshold = 3
```

The result will be (63, 8, 4), (63, 56, 54), and (80, 14, 9), with only three-node cliques found; see also Figure 5.4 for their graphical copies.

5.8 Providing Awareness by Higher-Level Knowledge on the Distributed System

In this section we will be consider some more diverse knowledge on the network of Figure 5.1, which may be grouped, averaged, summarized, or even effectively inferred in order to obtain higher-level awareness and assessment of the distributed system or its parts.

- **Evaluating the total length of the global communication network**

This will take into account the physical distances between its nodes on both sides of the existing links.

```
output _ sum(hop _ nodes(all, TYPE = global);
             hop _ links _ all(gc);
             PREDECESSOR < NAME; far(BEFORE, WHERE))
```

- **List all working collectives with the nodes each of them includes**

This starting from top manager nodes and collecting all nodes-departments under their control

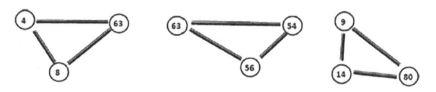

Figure 5.4   Resultant cliques in a global communication network.

```
output(
  hop _ first _ nodes(TYPE = global);
  unit(repeat(done(NAME), hop _ first _ links(wr))))
```

Result: $(\mathbf{34}, 1, 32, \ldots), (\mathbf{79}, 58, 77, \ldots), (\mathbf{48}, 43, 16, \ldots), (\mathbf{17}, 7, 35, \ldots),$
$(\mathbf{20}, 50, 69, \ldots), (\mathbf{82}, 72, 83, \ldots), (\mathbf{47}, 27, 30, \ldots), (\mathbf{51}, 11, 21, \ldots),$
$(\mathbf{74}, 25, 75, \ldots).$

- **Which working collective has the maximum number of offices**

```
output _ max(
  hop _ nodes(all, Type = top);
  append(count(repeat(done(stay), hop _ first _ links(wr))),
  NAME))
```

The result using the top manager's name as the name of the whole collective will be 20 or 82, as both have 12 constituent nodes.

- **Outline X_Y area occupied by the whole distributed system**

```
output(extend((Xmin, Xmax, Ymin, Ymax), (hop _ nodes(all);
  WHERE)))
```

The result is based on a very simple procedure (easily written when needed) extending all collected individual node addresses into the whole area minimally covering them all.

The returned result on the whole area will be represented as: Xmin = . . . , Xmax = . . . , Ymin = . . . , Ymax = . . .

- **Showing top business cooperation network between different organizations as a whole**

This will be inferred from existing inter-business links between some departments of different organizations. The resultant network may be represented by new business cooperation links bc (see Figure 5.2) between these organizations, which are symbolically represented by their top management nodes.

```
output(hop _ nodes(all); TYPE = top; COLOR = NAME;
       hop _ first(stay);
       unit(NAME, (fringe(repeat(done(stay),
       hop _ first _ links(wr)));
```

```
hop _ first _ links(all, ibl);
repeat(if((TYPE == top; done(NAME)),
      hop _ first _ links(wr))))))
```

The textual result will be as follows, where each bracketed group starts with the organization name as its top manager followed by other organizations (also named by top managers) directly linked to the start by new links: (**34**, 79, 17, 20), (**79**, 34, 17, 48, 20), (**48**, 79, 82), (**17**, 34, 79, 20, 47), (**20**, 34, 17, 79, 82, 51), (**82**, 48, 20, 74), (**47**, 17, 51), (**51**, 20, 47, 74), (**74**, 51, 82).

From this textual notation its graphical representation can be easily obtained, as shown in Figure 5.5.

5.9 Conclusions

Having provided a review of different meanings of awareness and existing approaches for its expression and support, the chapter investigated application of the developed Spatial Grasp Model and Technology for providing very practical awareness solutions in large distributed dynamic systems, with obtaining any knowledge needed

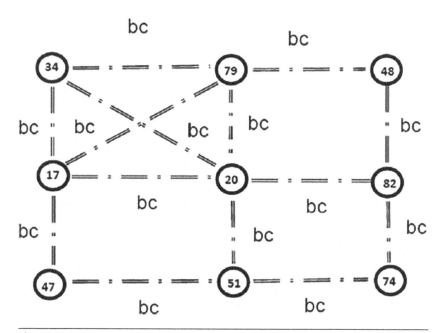

Figure 5.5 Resultant top business cooperation network.

from any point inside or outside the system. All presented exemplary solutions are very compact, highly parallel, and fully distributed, without the need of using vulnerable centralized resources. This may be explained by the completely different philosophy and ideology of SGT, which is not based on traditional systems partitioning and multiple agents communications (the latter essentially stemming from the "Society of Mind" approach [34]). On the contrary, SGT and its basic language supervise and control distributed systems by self-spreading and self-matching holistic recursive code in wavelike mode, which accumulates ultimate power in itself rather in the system its supervises. This may be conceptually closer even to some existing ideas of "soul" (for example, as in [35]), with obtained solutions that are much stronger, clearer, and more compact than with any other approaches.

References

1. Awareness. https://en.wikipedia.org/wiki/Awareness
2. What Is Spatial Awareness? https://numeracyforallab.ca/what-we-learned/developing-spatial-awareness/
3. Total Information Awareness. https://en.wikipedia.org/wiki/Total_Information_Awareness
4. R. Mohanan, What Are Distributed Systems? Architecture Types, Key Components, and Examples, 12 January 2022. www.spiceworks.com/tech/cloud/articles/what-is-distributed-computing/
5. P. M. Salmon, K. L. Plant, Distributed Situation Awareness: From Awareness in Individuals and Teams to the Awareness of Technologies, Sociotechnical Systems, and Societies, Applied Ergonomics, 2022, 98, 103599. www.sciencedirect.com/science/article/abs/pii/S0003687021002465
6. N. A. Stanton, Distributed Situation Awareness, Contemporary Ergonomics and Human Factors. In Charles, R., Wilkinson, J. (Eds.), CIEHF, 2016. https://publications.ergonomics.org.uk/uploads/Distributed-Situation-Awareness.pdf
7. M. M. Chatzimichailidou, A. Protopapas, I. M. Dokas, Seven Issues on Distributed Situation Awareness Measurement in Complex Sociotechnical Systems. In Boulanger, F., Krob, D., Morel, G., Roussel, J. C. (Eds.), Complex Systems Design & Management. Cham: Springer, 2015. https://doi.org/10.1007/978-3-319-11617-4_8. https://link.springer.com/chapter/10.1007/978-3-319-11617-4_8
8. E. Sultanov, E. Weber, Real World Awareness in Distributed Organizations: A View on Informal Processes, 2011. www.researchgate.net/publication/234720130_Real_World_Awareness_in_Distributed_Organizations_A_View_on_Informal_Processes

9. P. M. Salmon, N. A. Stanton, D. P. Jenkins, Distributed Situation Awareness Theory, Measurement and Application to Teamwork, By Copyright 2009, Published March 31, 2017 by CRC Press. www.routledge.com/Distributed-Situation-Awareness-Theory-Measurement-and-Application-to/Salmon-Stanton-Jenkins/p/book/9781138073852

10. M. M. Chatzimichailidou, R. Freund, I. Dokas, Distributed Situation Awareness as a "Middleware" Between the New Economic Sociology and Embedded Open Innovation. 6th International Conference on Mass Customization and Personalization in Central Europe (MCP-CE 2014). https://mcp-ce.org/wp-content/uploads/proceedings/2014/6_chatzimichailidou.pdf

11. J. S. Preden, J. Helander, Context Awareness in Distributed Computing Systems, Annales Univ. Sci. Budapest., Sect. Comp., 2009, 31, 57–73. www.researchgate.net/publication/255564252_Context_Awareness_in_Distributed_Computing_Systems

12. S. Jones, E. Milner, M. Sooriyabandara, S. Hauert, Distributed Situational Awareness in Robot Swarms, Advanced Intelligent Systems, 2020, 2. https://onlinelibrary.wiley.com/doi/10.1002/aisy.202000110

13. S. K. Gan, Z. Xu, S. Sukkarieh, Distributed Situational Awareness and Control, UAS Multi-Vehicle Cooperation and Coordination, 13 June 2016. https://onlinelibrary.wiley.com/doi/full/10.1002/9780470686652.eae1133

14. L. Ge, Y. Li, J. Yan, Y. Sun, Smart Distribution Network Situation Awareness for High-Quality Operation and Maintenance: A Brief Review, Energies, 2022, 15(3), 828. https://doi.org/10.3390/en15030828

15. J. Tanveer, A. Haider, R. Ali, A. Kim, An Overview of Reinforcement Learning Algorithms for Handover Management in 5G Ultra-Dense Small Cell Networks, Applied Sciences, 2022, 12(1), 426. https://doi.org/10.3390/app12010426 www.mdpi.com/2076-3417/12/1/426

16. P. S. Sapaty, A Distributed Processing System, European Patent N 0389655, Publ. 10.11.93. European Patent Office.

17. P. S. Sapaty, Mobile Processing in Distributed and Open Environments. New York: John Wiley & Sons, 1999.

18. P. S. Sapaty, Ruling Distributed Dynamic Worlds. New York: John Wiley & Sons, 2005.

19. P. S. Sapaty, Managing Distributed Dynamic Systems with Spatial Grasp Technology. Springer, 2017.

20. P. S. Sapaty, Holistic Analysis and Management of Distributed Social Systems. Springer, 2018.

21. P. S. Sapaty, Complexity in International Security: A Holistic Spatial Approach. Emerald Publishing, 2019.

22. P. S. Sapaty, Symbiosis of Real and Simulated Worlds under Spatial Grasp Technology. Springer, 2021.

23. P. S. Sapaty, Spatial Grasp as a Model for Space-based Control and Management Systems. CRC Press, 2022.

24. P. S. Sapaty, The Spatial Grasp Model: Applications and Investigations of Distributed Dynamic Worlds. Emerald Publishing, 2023.

25. P. S. Sapaty, Distributed Control Technology for Air and Missile Defence Operations, International Relations and Diplomacy, 2022, 10(4), 141–157. https://doi.org/10.17265/2328-2134/2022.04.001. www.davidpublisher.com/Public/uploads/Contribute/6364741a7b432.pdf
26. P. S. Sapaty, Relation of Spatial Grasp Paradigm to Higher Psychological and Mental Concepts, Acta Scientific Computer Sciences, 2022, 4(12). https://actascientific.com/ASCS/pdf/ASCS-04-0359.pdf
27. P. S. Sapaty, Seeing and Managing Distributed Worlds with Spatial Grasp Paradigm, Acta Scientific Computer Sciences, 2022, 4(12). https://actascientific.com/ASCS/pdf/ASCS-04-0365.pdf
28. P. S. Sapaty, Comprehending Distributed Worlds with the Spatial Grasp Paradigm, Mathematical Machines and Systems, 2022, 1. www.immsp.kiev.ua/publications/articles/2022/2022_1/01_22_Sapaty.pdf
29. P. S. Sapaty, Spatial Management of Air and Missile Defence Operations, Mathematical Machines and Systems, 2023, 1. www.immsp.kiev.ua/publications/articles/2023/2023_1/01_23_Sapaty.pdf
30. P. S. Sapaty, Providing Distributed System Integrity under Spatial Grasp Technology, Mathematical Machines and Systems, 2023, 2. www.immsp.kiev.ua/publications/articles/2023/2023_2/02_23_Sapaty.pdf
31. P. S. Sapaty, Providing Global Awareness in Distributed Dynamic Systems, International Relations and Diplomacy, 2023, 11(2), 87–100. https://doi.org/10.17265/2328-2134/2023.02.002. www.davidpublisher.com/Public/uploads/Contribute/6486c3d05a6cc.pdf
32. P. S. Sapaty, Simulating Distributed Consciousness with Spatial Grasp Model, Mathematical Machines and Systems, 2023, 3.
33. P. S. Sapaty, Managing Distributed Systems with Spatial Grasp Patterns, Mathematical Machines and Systems, 2023, 4.
34. M. Minsky, The Society of Mind, Simon & Schuster, 1988.
35. N. Hodgkinson, Who Is Thinking: The Soul or the Brain? The Daily Guardian, 29 August 2020. https://thedailyguardian.com/who-is-thinking-the-soul-or-the-brain/

6

SIMULATING DISTRIBUTED CONSCIOUSNESS WITH SPATIAL GRASP MODEL

6.1 Introduction

The aim of this chapter is to investigate the applicability and efficiency of Spatial Grasp Model and Technology, which has been developed and tested on numerous applications for expressing and simulating different ideas and capabilities of this mysterious and so far almost unknown feature called consciousness. This has been accomplished despite numerous ideas of its existence and location, often controversial and fantastic, which have been offered and published for centuries. And this work is particularly oriented towards obtaining consciousness features in large distributed and dynamic systems, which may cover economy, ecology, security, and defense, as well as may other areas. The rest of the chapter is organized as follows. Section 6.2 reviews existing works and publications on consciousness grouped by the following categories: definition and theory of consciousness, modes of consciousness, artificial consciousness, origin and features of consciousness, spreading and outside consciousness, gestalt and pattern-based consciousness, consciousness and control, conscious and subconscious processes, collective consciousness, simulating consciousness by the Spatial Grasp Model, consciousness in psychology and psychiatry, and international consciousness. Section 6.3 reviews the main ideas of the Spatial Grasp Model and Technology and its Spatial Grasp Language, described in Chapters 2 and 3. Section 6.4 shows a very simple example in SGL for organizing and managing a swarm of chasers searching for scattered targets on different levels: discovering and eliminating targets on the shooting distance, sharing the seen targets with neighboring swarm members by embedded distributed awareness, and finally providing higher awareness and related to consciousness capabilities. Section 6.5 discusses potential capabilities of having awareness and even consciousness of the whole country, by representing it as integrity of vital components like economy, society, defense, ecology, and government. It shows some elementary examples in SGL which may relate to different components, like finding network images in pattern matching mode, outlining a specific region, and broadcasting executive orders via satellite network. Finally, some consciousness-related features are discussed using obtained summary estimates from different components, like generating important global feelings and opinions that may influence the current and future development of the whole system and showing the implementation of global consciousness under SGT in a fully distributed and self-wandering way. Section 6.6 contains a summary on investigated potential application of SGT for different consciousness categories mentioned in Section 6.2, like global workspace, knowing-feeling-acting, gestalt and pattern-based consciousness, origin and features of consciousness, spreading and outside consciousness, collective consciousness, and international consciousness. Section 6.7 concludes the chapter with a strong belief in the potential applicability of the developed spatial model and technology for expressing and simulating different consciousness features in a variety of important distributed and dynamic systems. References include many analyzed sources on different consciousness features, as well as existing publications on SGT and its applications that proved particularly useful for the conducted analysis.

6.2 Review of Existing Works on Consciousness

- **Definition and theory of consciousness**

  Consciousness, at its simplest, is sentience and awareness of internal and external existence [1]. However, its nature has led to millennia of analyses, explanations, and debates by philosophers, theologians, linguists, and scientists. Opinions differ about what exactly needs to be studied or what is even considered consciousness. In some explanations, it is synonymous with the mind, and at other times, an aspect of mind.

The *hard problem of consciousness* asks why and how humans have qualia or phenomenal experiences [2]. This is in contrast to the "easy problems" of explaining the physical systems that give humans and other animals the ability to discriminate, integrate information, and so forth. Such problems are called easy because all that is required for their solution is to specify the mechanisms that perform such functions.

Evolution has been the unifying theory of biology, but consciousness is rarely studied in the context of evolution [3]. Its theories come from religion, philosophy, and cognitive science, but not much from evolutionary biology. The offered theory suggests that consciousness arises as a solution to the problem facing any nervous system: too much information constantly flows in to be fully processed.

The term *consciousness has eluded a precise definition for thousands of years* [4]. Summary definitions of it fall short when it comes to capturing the dimensionality of the term. We might use the word consciousness to describe perceptual awareness, the nature of being awake and alert, or self-awareness and intentionality.

The conscious system is an open and dynamic one, interacting with the environment [5]. It is composed of three functions: knowing, feeling, and acting. Human consciousness is dynamically constituted by the interactions between the three functions in time cycles.

- **Models of consciousness**

Models of consciousness are used to illustrate and aid in understanding and explaining distinctive aspects of consciousness [6]. Sometimes the models are labeled theories of consciousness. There are different types of models, including mathematical, logical, verbal, and conceptual models.

A model of consciousness is a theoretical description that relates the brain properties of consciousness (e.g. fast irregular electrical activity, widespread brain activation) to phenomenal properties of consciousness [7]. Because of the diverse nature of these properties, useful models can be either mathematical/ logical or verbal/conceptual.

A mathematical model of embodied consciousness is introduced that is based on the hypothesis that the spatial field of consciousness is structured by a projective geometry and under the control of a process of active inference [8]. This combines multisensory evidence with prior beliefs in memory and frames them by selecting points of view and perspectives according to preferences.

- **Artificial consciousness**

Artificial consciousness, also known as machine consciousness or synthetic consciousness, is a field related to artificial intelligence and cognitive robotics [9]. Neuroscience hypothesizes that consciousness is generated by the interoperation of various parts of the brain, though there are challenges to that perspective.

The work [10] provides *new insights into artificial intelligence (AI) and machine consciousness*, with the perspective of AI added to this book edition. It shows that contemporary AI has a hidden problem that prevents it from becoming a true intelligent agent. A self-evident solution to the problem is given in this book.

Replication or even modeling of consciousness in machines requires some clarifications and refinements of our concept of consciousness [11]. Design of, construction of, and interaction with artificial systems can itself assist in this conceptual development. This activity may in turn nurture the development of our concepts of consciousness.

The work [12] introduces the *concept of a virtual "global workspace"* that emerges by connecting different brain areas to describe consciousness. In global workspace theory, consciousness arises from specific types of information-processing computations, which are physically realized by the hardware of the brain.

- **Origin and features of consciousness**

The work [13] analyzes whether higher *spatial dimensions may hold the key to solving the hard problem of consciousness*. The hard problem of consciousness is the most pressing unsolved mystery in both philosophy and science. To solve such a problem, we are going to need revolutionary ways of thinking. There exist arguments that higher spatial dimensions might hold the key to the hard problem.

How *brain waves may create consciousness* is discussed in [14]. At the root of all our thoughts, emotions, and behaviors is the communication between neurons within our brains. Brain waves are produced by synchronized electrical pulses from masses of neurons communicating with each other, and a brain wave is a repetitive or rhythmic neural activity in the brain. Brain waves are classified with different frequencies. Consciousness is considered a function of these frequencies.

To explain *consciousness as a physical process* we must acknowledge the role of energy in the brain [15]. Energetic activity is fundamental to all physical processes and causally drives biological behavior. Recent neuroscientific evidence can be interpreted in a way that suggests consciousness is a product of the organization of energetic activity in the brain.

- **Spreading and outside consciousness**

Spreading consciousness and awareness in the brain is discussed in [16]. Brain-scan images are iridescent icons of today's science of the mind. Molecular changes inside the skulls are transformed into images sporting multicolored splotches signifying pockets of heightened brain activity. These neural patches may be considered the products of specialized brain structures that coordinate the mental process.

Whether consciousness can exist outside of the brain is discussed in [17]. The prevailing consensus in neuroscience is that consciousness is an emergent property of the brain, and when the brain dies, the mind and consciousness of the being to whom that brain belonged cease to exist. Bus some researchers now believe that consciousness persists after death and exists independently and outside of the brain.

What if consciousness is not an emergent property of the brain is discussed in [18]. The assumption within today's neuroscience is that all aspects of consciousness arise solely from interactions among neurons in the brain. But if consciousness entails more than the activity of neurons, then we can contemplate new ways of thinking about it. This review examines phenomena where consciousness extends beyond the physical brain and body in both space and time.

Whether consciousness and the world may be one is discussed in [19]. No convincing account has been presented of exactly where and how consciousness is stored in our bodies. Yet consciousness is real, and, like any other real phenomenon, is physical. The authors propose a radical hypothesis that consciousness is one and the same as the physical world surrounding us.

The idea of science of mind wandering, empirically navigating the stream of consciousness, is discussed in [20]. Conscious experience is fluid; it rarely remains on one topic for an extended period without deviation. Its dynamic nature is illustrated by the experience of mind wandering, in which attention switches from a current task to unrelated thoughts and feelings.

- **Gestalt and pattern-based consciousness**

The work in *gestalt often facilitates accessing what is held subconscious,* and the client sometimes moves into an altered state of consciousness, as in [21]. It releases the subconscious mind from what is trapped there and encourages the full body and every cell to release pain. We become healthy in body, mind, spirit, and emotions as the process unfolds.

Linking consciousness with pattern recognition is covered in [22]. It is a phenomenological proof that pattern-recognition and subjective consciousness are the same activity in different terms. Therefore, it proves that essential subjective processes of consciousness are computable and identifies significant traits and requirements of a conscious system.

Patterns for consciousness are discussed in [23]. Anyone who succeeds in business or society knows how to interact with complex human systems. They are able to see patterns, make sense of them, and choose. They act and make a difference for themselves and others. Whether they focus on family, team, organization, community, or nation, individuals and groups influence each other.

An *introduction to patterns of the consciousness* is covered in [24]. Human consciousness naturally develops patterns as a way to be effective in its functioning in receiving, processing, storing, retrieving, and transmitting information. This effectiveness is crucial for survival, especially for our ancestors, when they needed to respond to potential threats in a timely manner.

The idea that consciousness is a thing, not a process, is discussed in [25]. The central dogma of cognitive psychology is consciousness is a process, not a thing. The paper's opinion, however, is that conscious sensory experiences are not processes at all. They are things: specifically, *spatial electromagnetic patterns,* which in principle could be generated by hardware rather than wetware.

- **Consciousness and control**

Representation of *consciousness as control and controlled perception* is covered in [26]. The brain is considered a control system with its organization and functioning described and implications for the way we consider consciousness discussed. A phenomenon proposed by a massively interconnected network of sophisticated control systems that can produce language, imagine, plan, and do many other things.

> *Conscious control over action* is discussed in [27]. The extensive involvement of nonconscious processes in human behavior has led some to suggest that consciousness is much less important for the control of action than we might think. This article pushes against this trend, developing an understanding of conscious control that is sensitive to our best models of overt action control.

The slogan *"I Am Conscious, Therefore, I Am"* is discussed in [28]. Organisms are adapted to each other and the environment because there is an inbuilt striving toward security, stability, and equilibrium. A general theory of behavior connects imagery, affect, and action with the *central executive system we call consciousness.* This assumes that primary motivation of consciousness and intentional behavior is psychological homeostasis.

- **Conscious and subconscious processes**

Conscious and subconscious processes of the human mind are discussed and compared in [29]. Conscious processing is partially done by unconscious processes, and analysis of a vast amount of information occurs outside of awareness. Consciousness has got some advantages that the unconscious does not. Previous studies have shown that people are consciously aware of their implicit evaluations.

- **Collective consciousness**

Collective consciousness, collective conscience, or collective consciousis the set of shared beliefs, ideas, and moral attitudes that operate as a unifying force within society [30]. Rather than existing as separate individuals, people come together as dynamic groups to share resources and knowledge. The modern concept of what can be considered collective consciousness includes solidarity attitudes, memes, extreme behaviors like group-think and herd behavior, and collectively shared experiences during collective rituals and dance parties.

- **Simulating consciousness by the Spatial Grasp Model**

Paper [31] investigates the possibility of using Spatial Grasp model and technology (SGT) that has been developed and tested in different countries for *simulating global awareness and consciousness in distributed dynamic systems*, with potential applications in intelligent system management, industrial development, space research, security, and defense.

Paper [32] shows how to *simulate distributed and global consciousness* using Spatial Grasp Language, allowing us to obtain compact spatial solutions by directly expressing their top semantics. It first describes a traditional organization of two conflicting swarms (called chasers and targets), and then effectively enriches the chasers with global battlefield awareness and consciousness.

Presentation [33] briefs Spatial Grasp Technology equally working with physical, virtual, and combined spaces and applications including network theory, missile defense, collective robotics, command and control, and industrial, social, and security problems. It shows how this model can be useful in understanding and simulating complex awareness and consciousness features.

- ### Consciousness in psychology and psychiatry

How *consciousness may relate to psychology* is presented in [34]. Consciousness is the individual awareness of your unique thoughts, memories, feelings, sensations, and environments. Your conscious experiences are constantly shifting and changing. Next, for example, you might notice how uncomfortable your chair is, or maybe you are mentally planning dinner.

> *Consciousness in psychology, theories, and examples* is discussed in [35]. Consciousness is not found lying in physics equations or peering at us from the periodic table. Somehow, it materializes out of the nervous system and endows us with the ability to be aware, have self-knowledge, and hold a set of emotions and beliefs about both the environment and ourselves.

Article [36] takes a look at the different meanings given to the notion of consciousness and shows how *abandoning psychopathological controversies* can lead to shallowness in the understanding of psychiatric pathology. It also highlights how different philosophical doctrines and psychological theories can be traced in every point of view, which approaches the phenomenon of consciousness.

> *Psychiatric definition of consciousness* (as in [37]): it is the ability to be aware of oneself as an individual in relation to the surrounding world; the ability to correctly interpret one's own experiences. If the ability to self-identify or experience experiences is "altered," then it can lead to "qualitative disorder."

- ### International consciousness

The problem of *international peace* is not materially different from the problem of peace in the individual, the community, or the nation [38]. It is a question in part at least of a state of mind. "As a man thinks in his heart so is he" is as true of nations as of individuals. We can never be sure of world peace until we get an organization of international sentiment that will make for peace. The international conscience is therefore the ultimate guarantee of international peace.

6.3 Spatial Grasp Model and Technology Basics

This section reviews only key ideas of the basic model and technology that may be useful to comprehend more quickly the material of this chapter, with technology details in Chapters 2 and 3 and more in [31–33, 39–55]. Within Spatial Grasp Model and Technology, a high-level operational scenario is represented as an active self-evolving pattern rather than a traditional program. This pattern expressed in recursive Spatial Grasp Language, starting at any world point (or points), propagates, replicates, modifies, covers, and matches the distributed environment in parallel wavelike mode. This propagation also combines feedback echoing of the reached control states and obtained data, which may be remote, for making higher-level decisions, altogether providing holistic solutions unachievable by other models and systems. SGL allows for expressing direct space presence and operations with unlimited parallelism. Its universal recursive organization with operational scenarios called *grasp* can be expressed just by a single string:

$$grasp \quad \rightarrow \quad constant \mid variable \mid rule \; (\{grasp,\})$$

The SGL *rule* expresses certain action, control, description, or context accompanied with operands, which can themselves be any *grasp* too. Each SGL interpreter copy can handle and process multiple active SGL scenario code, which is freely evolving and propagating in space and between the interpreters.

6.4 Distributed Management up to Spatial Consciousness

This describes the organization of a swarm of chasers aimed at destroying distributed targets on some expected area. We will consider the situation where the chasers are constantly moving, searching for, and destroying scattered targets that happen to appear at a shooting distance.

- **Discovering targets at the shooting distance and destroying them**

The following scenario, activating all chasers in parallel, will be doing this, with chasers operating independently from each other; see also Figure 6.1.

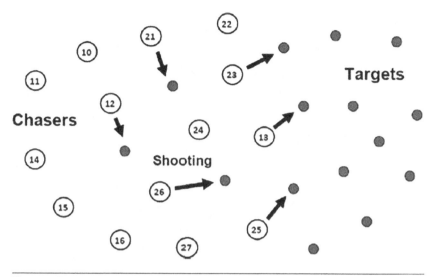

Figure 6.1   The swarm of chasers attacking hostile targets on an expected area.

```
hop _ chasers(all); nodal(Area = . . .);
repeat(if(seen(targets),
          select _ move _ destroy(target),
          move _ random(Area)))
```

- **Collecting targets seen and sharing them with other swarm members**

This works like embedded distributed awareness of all targets seen somehow by individual chasers. In the case of not having targets at a shooting distance, individual chasers can at least try to move towards the regions where potential targets are currently located, in hope to reach and shoot some eventually. And in the worst case, they can just move again in a blind and random fashion, as in the previous case. This can be expressed in SGL as follows; see also Figure 6.2.

```
hop _ chasers(all); nodal(Area = . . ., Global);
repeat(enrich(Global, search(targets _ seen));
       enrich((hop(all _ neighbors); Global), Global);
       or _ seq(select _ move _ destroy(Global),
               select _ move(Global),
               move _ random(Area)))
```

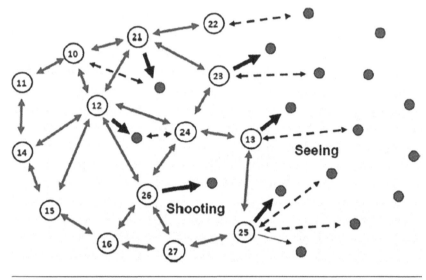

Figure 6.2 Embedded distributed awareness of all targets seen locally.

- **Introducing higher awareness, command, control, and consciousness levels**

This involves collecting all targets in the operational area using a specialized high-resolution, long-distance vision system and enhancing the global data awareness of individual chasers, assisting them in panning movements towards potential targets. It also involves assessing the global situation based on the current numbers of chasers and targets, extending the region they are operating on, and making higher-level recommendations and decisions on the whole mission. This can be accomplished by introducing a special global awareness, assessment, and feeling level close to the idea of consciousness (such higher-level capabilities may be permanently *system-embedded*, *freely migrating* over the chasers bodies, or *outside ones* like owned by another system); see also Figure 6.3. The following higher-level features may be possible in this direction.

a. *Global awareness and management*: collecting all targets by a higher-level observation system, enriching all actively and independently operating chasers with extended global data covering all operational areas.

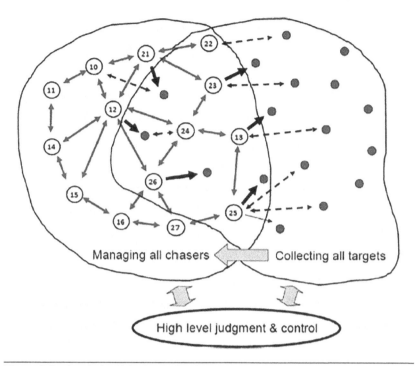

Figure 6.3   Introducing higher-level collection, management, awareness, and consciousness levels.

```
frontal(Targ _ all); nodal(Area) = . . .;
repeat(stay(Targ _ all = collect(targets, Area);
          hop _ chasers(all); enrich(Global, Targ _ all));
     sleep(delay))
```

b. *Generating feelings about the campaign rationale* based on current global dynamic numbers, with recommendations of their increasing or decreasing.

```
Chasers _ numb = count(hop _ chasers(all));
Targets _ numb = count(collect(targets, Area));
If(Chasers _ numb < Targets _ numb,
increase(Chasers _ numb, Area),
decrease(Chasers _ numb, Area))
```

c. *More complex assessment and feeling* including current chasers and targets numbers, their comparison, and extension of the operational area, which may recommend even termination of the whole campaign as useless or too dangerous, believably altogether closer to a sort of *global operational consciousness.*

```
Chasers _ numb = count(hop _ chasers(all));
Targets _ numb = count(collect(targets, Area));
if(and(Chasers _ numb / Targets _ numb < Threshold1,
        Chasers _ numb <= Threshold2,
        Targets _ numb > Threshold3,
        coverage(Area) > Threshold4)),
    or(reduce(Area), increase(Chasers _ numb),
terminate(campaign)))
```

6.5 Global Awareness and Consciousness of the Whole Society

As already mentioned in Section 6.2, *collective consciousness* is the set of shared beliefs, ideas, and moral attitudes that operate as a unifying force within society [30]. Also, *international consciousness* may not be fundamentally different from the consciousness in an individual, community, or nation [38]. We will be discussing here in brief how SGT can be useful to express, simulate, and practically support higher-level organization up to global consciousness of the whole country. The latter can be symbolically represented as interaction of its key components strongly depending from and critically influencing each other, as shown in Figure 6.4.

The following is, in brief, what the components of Figure 6.7 really mean, with references to the related theoretical and practical problems being investigated and tested by SGT for a long period and in different countries.

6.5.1 Economy

This combines various institutions, agencies, entities, decision-making processes, and patterns of consumption that comprise the economic structure of a given community. Such structure includes transportation and communications systems, industrial facilities, education and technology, housing markets, goods markets, and different banks,

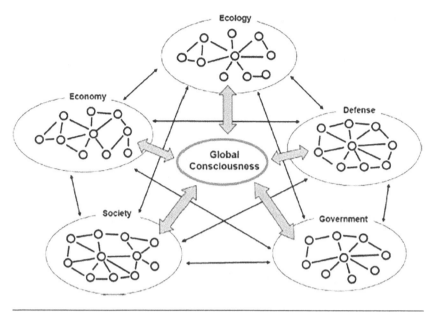

Figure 6.4 Representation of the whole country as interaction and cooperation of its key components.

which enable a country or region to produce goods, services, and other resources. See related management examples in SGL in [42].

6.5.2 Society

Societies are often characterized by social structures that include family, religion, law, economy, and class. This often contrasts with the notion of social system that refers to the parent structure in which these various structures are embedded. Social structures significantly influence larger systems, such as economic systems, legal systems, political systems, and cultural systems. Solving social problems in SGL may be found in [43].

6.5.3 Defense

Defense is usually linked with the armed forces, which are divided into three military branches: army, navy, and air force. Internal security forces, like gendarmeries, military police, and security forces, paramilitary forces, militia, internal troops, and police tactical units, are an internal security service common in most of the world. Different defense-related examples in SGL are covered in [41, 44, 46].

6.5.4 Ecology

The ecosystem consists of terrestrial and aquatic ecosystems. The terrestrial ecosystem includes forest ecosystem, desert ecosystem, mountain ecosystem, grassland ecosystem, and tundra ecosystem. Aquatic are ecosystems that represent a body of water. These can be further divided into freshwater ecosystem and marine ecosystem. Examples of ecology-related solutions under SGT are presented in [42, 47].

6.5.5 Government

Government consists of executive bodies, judiciary, and legislature. The executive often includes the president, deputy president, and cabinet ministers at a national level and the premier and members of the executive councils at a provincial level. Judicial authority is vested in the courts, which are independent and subject to the laws of the constitution. Legislature means a body of elected representatives that makes laws needed for the government and the country to function. See related solutions in SGL in [42, 44, 46].

- **Elementary examples of spatial SGL solutions**

  We are showing here only some elementary examples in SGL confirming efficiency and simplicity of their expression under the Spatial Grasp paradigm (which are described in full details in the mentioned SGT-oriented publications). These may relate to the workspace connecting different brain areas (as in [12]), the unconscious and subconscious levels (like in [29]), as well as the knowing and acting functionalities (as in [5]).

    a. *Processing network images.* This example relates to spatial seeing of fully distributed networks and finding proper images-structures in them like the one in Figure 6.5a, which may represent a two-level specific control hierarchy where additionally all its bottom nodes are fully interconnected with each other. A network with a positive match of the Figure 6.5a

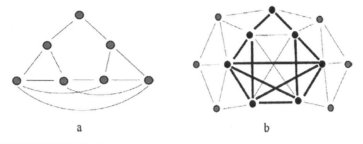

Figure 6.5 Pattern matching in a distributed network: (a) image to be found; (b) network with positive match.

structure is shown in Figure 6.5b, which may be obtained by the following self-matching SGL pattern reflecting the image in Figure 6.5a, as follows, with the match confirmed if found.

```
hop _ area(. . .);
hop _ nodes(all); COLOR = NAME;
frontal(Fringe) = (hop _ first(links, all);
                   hop _ first(links, all); NAME);
if(and _ parallel(
     (hop _ nodes _ all(Fringe); remove(NAME, Fringe);
      and _ parallel(hop(link(any), nodes _ all(Fringe))))),
   output("match found"))
```

b. *Finding region border coordinates.* The self-evolving virus-like SGL code spreading in parallel via the expected fire area picks up and returns coordinates of the reached border points, issuing the final image of the region (say, representing forest fire) after collecting enough border coordinates (see Figure 6.6, also [48–50] for detailed description of such examples).

```
frontal(Zone _ color = . . ., Branches = . . ., Start = . . .);
hop(Start); nodal(Border);
parallel(
    (hop _ node(any, equal(COLOR, Zone _ color));
     repeat(
       replicate(Branches, shift _ random(dx _ dy));
               if(nonequal(COLOR, Zone _ color),
                   done(append((hop(Start); Border),
       WHERE)))))),
    (sleep(. . .); output(Border)))
```

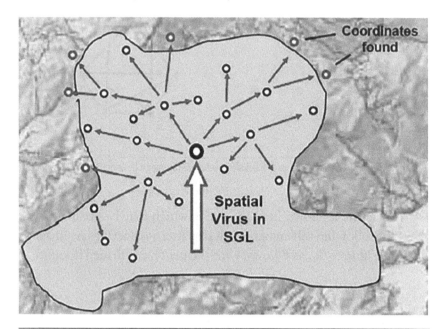

Figure 6.6   Parallel outlining the border coordinates of a forest fire region.

c. *Broadcasting executive orders to a satellite network.* Starting from the first reached satellite from ground station G1, the following scenario is broadcasting the given order to all other satellites via their dynamic network, while blocking possible propagation cycles, as in Figure 6.7. Each reached satellite executes the order brought to it in frontal variable Order, whereas the parallel wavelike scenario simultaneously spreads to the neighboring nodes.

```
frontal(Order) = instructions;
hop(G1); hop _ first _ any _ sat(seen);
repeat(free(execute(Order)),hop _ first _ all _ sat(seen))
```

- **Expressing higher awareness and consciousness features**

For such enormously large, highly developed, massively interconnected and globally controlled distributed systems as in Figure 6.4, we can offer an unlimited number of local and global understanding, assessment, coordination, modification, and management scenarios, which may reflect a sort of symbiosis of their global awareness (like, say, in [53]) and distributed and global consciousness. Next, we show only some of such awareness-consciousness solutions.

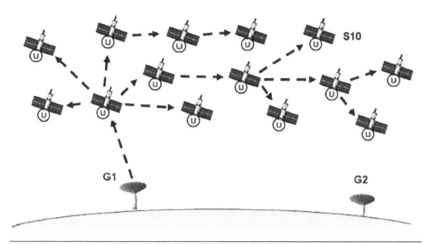

Figure 6.7 Delivery executive orders via satellite network in a self-flooding mode.

a. *Obtaining some global numbers*:

```
Production_all=sum(hop_area(Economy);hop_nodes(all);
    PRODUCE);
Consumption_all =
    sum(hop_areas(Economy, Society, Government, Defense,
    Ecology);
        hop_nodes(all); CONSUME);
```

b. *Providing resultant global opinion and advice*:

```
Above = Production_all—Consumption_all;
if(Above < zero, conduct(state-borrowing), OK);
```

c. *Achieving integral global feeling and recommendation*:

```
Consumption_mil = sum(hop_area(Defense); hop_nodes(all);
    CONSUME);
Defense_share = (Consumption_mil / Production_all) * 100;
If(and(Defense_share<2, Above>0), improve(Defense))
```

- **Wandering consciousness**

In the previous examples we assumed that the model of global consciousness works in a centralized way, as in Figure 6.4. But the unique flexibility of SGT, which can self-spread, self-cover, and self-match distributed environments, also allows us to organize a sort of independent and freely wandering solutions, like matching the ideas of

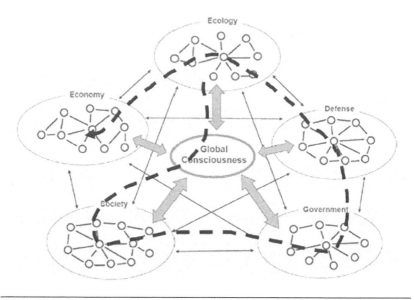

Figure 6.8 Wandering global consciousness.

[16–20], which can operate independently, in parallel, and even in a superior way to the previous centralized case, as symbolically shown in Figure 6.8.

In the following scenario, the point of consciousness concentration migrates in a random way between different system components, analyzes their financial states, and provides both local and global estimates and opinions for their improvements (randomly accessing centralized consciousness too). As in the previous example, we consider only financial characteristics, but in a similar way, simultaneously or even jointly, any other local and global system features can be investigated and evaluated too, like security, climate change, pandemics, education, culture, education, psychology, and so on.

```
fronral(Above _ global = initial, History);
nodal(Opinion);
repeat(hop _ random _ area(Ecology, Economy, Society,
         Government,Defense,Global_Consciousness);
      Above = sum(hop_nodes(all); PRODUCE - CONSUME);
      Opinion = assess(Above_global, Above, History);
   if(important(Opinion), recommend_action(Opinion));
      Above_global += Above ; update(History, Opinion))
```

6.6 Summary on Simulation of Different Consciousness Features in SGT

Detailed analysis of almost all existing consciousness concepts and ideas, like those discussed in Section 6.2 (reviewed from [1–38]), confirms the full applicability of SGT and its basic language SGL for their expression and implementation in fully distributed systems [39–53]. Some of these are mentioned as follows.

Global workspace emerges (see also [12]) by connecting different brain areas. This can be easily modeled in SGL by distributed physical-virtual networks with the existing and published repertoire of their creation, modification, and graph pattern-matching analyses.

Knowing, feeling, acting, representing composition of conscious system (as in [5]), also functioning of mind within a single brain as hierarchy of *conscious mind* (will power, planning, decisions, judgment), *subconscious mind* (long-term memory, emotions, creativity), and *unconscious mind* (with automatic control as in [29]). These can be expressed in SGL in a fully distributed manner while preserving the high integrity of separate components and their deep integration and symbiosis.

Gestalt and pattern-based consciousness [21–25]. Expressing subconscious and conscious levels based on gestalt psychology laws and pattern theory, allowing the human mind to grasp the whole first, can be effectively accomplished under SGT and SGL with the gained practical experience of doing related things in large, distributed, and dynamic systems with the use of active self-matching holistic images or patterns.

Origin and features of consciousness (like spatial dimensions, waves) [13, 14], where arguments that higher spatial dimensions might hold the key to the hard problem of consciousness [2], or consciousness is considered as a function of *brain waves* with different frequencies. All these ideas perfectly relate to the developed and tested Spatial Grasp Model and Technology, which is fundamentally based on self-spreading parallel waves under recursive spatial control. But this paradigm also supplies spreading waves with *additional power* as they can carry themselves unlimited spatial functionality, being much superior to the systems they cover and from which they can be independent.

Spreading and outside consciousness [16–20]. The dynamic nature of consciousness is illustrated by the experience of *mind wandering* in which attention often switches from a current task to unrelated thoughts and feelings. Some researchers even believe that *consciousness persists after death* and exists *independently and outside of the brain*. Others propose a radical hypothesis that consciousness is *one and the same as the physical world* surrounding us. All such hypotheses and ideas can be effectively expressed and implemented in SGL by creating powerful recursive scenarios that can unlimitedly self-spread, cover, match, create, and control both virtual and physical worlds, with numerous related examples already existing and published.

Collective consciousness, international consciousness [30, 38]. These represent the *set of shared beliefs*, ideas, and moral attitudes that operate as a unifying force within society. The problem of international peace is not materially different from the problem of peace in the individual, the community, or the nation. SGT has been used to describe numerous collective solutions, from group behavior of animals or robotic swarms to large social systems, international management, and security problems. Compact spatial SGL scenarios allow us to describe holistic distributed collective solutions on a high conceptual level and keep global control in complex situations, if needed.

6.7 Conclusions

We conclude this chapter with a strong belief of the potential applicability of the developed spatial model and technology for expressing and simulating consciousness ideas and features. The SGT can implement numerous consciousness hypotheses on a variety of levels, starting from *creating artificial neuron systems* with embedded network capabilities exchanging messages between neurons, to *simulating spreading waves between neurons*, to *representing consciousness as freely wandering* throughout and over the neuron structures, to fully *self-contained consciousness* outside of the brain, to its *existence independently in the whole world*, even preceding its creation. Self-evolving active scenarios in SGL can *keep all power and functionality* inside their autonomous evolution in distributed spaces with full capability of *expressing and simulating any consciousness ideas*. The described technology can be quickly implemented and tested on any platform, as was successfully experimented with in different countries with the author's engagement.

References

1. Consciousness. https://en.wikipedia.org/wiki/Consciousness
2. Hard Problem of Consciousness. https://en.wikipedia.org/wiki/Hard_problem_of_consciousness
3. M. Graziano, A New Theory Explains How Consciousness Evolved, The Atlantic, 6 June 2016. www.theatlantic.com/science/archive/2016/06/how-consciousness-evolved/485558/
4. K. Schultz, Consciousness: Definition, Examples, & Theory. The Berkeley Well-Being Institute, LLC, 2023. www.berkeleywellbeing.com/consciousness.html
5. A. Pereira Jr., The Projective Theory of Consciousness: From Neuroscience to Philosophical Psychology, Trans/Form/Ação, Marília, 2018, 41, 199–232, Edição Especial. www.scielo.br/j/trans/a/5xcwgRK9wtfkf4Wm48FKGfv/?format=pdf&lang=en
6. Models of Consciousness. https://en.wikipedia.org/wiki/Models_of_consciousness
7. A. Seth, Models of Consciousness, Scholarpedia, 2007, 2(1), 1328. www.scholarpedia.org/article/Models_of_consciousness
8. D. Rudrauf, D. Bennequin, I. Granic, G. Landini, K. Friston, K. Williford, A Mathematical Model of Embodied Consciousness, Journal of Theoretical Biology, 2017, 428, 106–131. www.sciencedirect.com/science/article/abs/pii/S0022519317302540
9. Artificial Consciousness. https://en.wikipedia.org/wiki/Artificial_consciousness
10. P. O. Haikonen, Consciousness and Robot Sentience (2nd Edition, Machine Consciousness). World Scientific, 2019. www.amazon.com/Consciousness-Robot-Sentience-2nd-Machine/dp/9811205043
11. A. Sloman, R. Chrisley, Virtual Machines and Consciousness, Journal of Consciousness Studies, 2003, 10(4–5). www.cs.bham.ac.uk/research/projects/cogaff/sloman-chrisley-jcs03.pdf
12. P. Krauss, A. Maier, Will We Ever Have Conscious Machines? Frontiers in Computational Neuroscience, 2020, 14. https://doi.org/10.3389/fncom.2020.556544. www.frontiersin.org/articles/10.3389/fncom.2020.556544/full
13. P. Sjöstedt-H, Consciousness and Higher Spatial Dimensions, 14 April 2022. https://iai.tv/articles/consciousness-and-higher-spatial-dimensions-auid-2107

14. T. Das, Brain Waves Create Consciousness, International Journal of Development Research, 2018, 8(6), 20910–20912. www.journalijdr.com/brain-waves-create-consciousness

15. R. Pepperell, Consciousness as a Physical Process Caused by the Organization of Energy in the Brain, Sec. Consciousness Research, 2018, 9. www.frontiersin.org/articles/10.3389/fpsyg.2018.02091/full

16. B. Bower, Spreading Consciousness, Awareness Goes Global in the Brain, Science News, 15 October 2002. www.sciencenews.org/article/spreading-consciousness

17. C. N. Lazarus, Can Consciousness Exist Outside of the Brain? The Brain May Not Create Consciousness But "Filter" It, Psychology Today, 26 June 2019. www.psychologytoday.com/intl/blog/think-well/201906/can-consciousness-exist-outside-the-brain

18. H. Wahbeh, D. Radin, C. Cannard, A. Delorme, What If Consciousness Is Not an Emergent Property of the Brain? Observational and Empirical Challenges to Materialistic Models, Frontiers in Psychology, 2022, 13. www.frontiersin.org/articles/10.3389/fpsyg.2022.955594/full

19. R. Manzotti, The Spread Mind: Why Consciousness and the World Are One. OR Books, 2018. www.amazon.com/Spread-Mind-Why-Consciousness-World/dp/1944869492

20. J. Smallwood, J. W. Schooler, The Science of Mind Wandering: Empirically Navigating the Stream of Consciousness, Annual Review of Psychology, 2015, 66, 487–518. https://pubmed.ncbi.nlm.nih.gov/25293689/

21. M. Pearce, Gestalt: Beyond the Conscious Mind, 2 May 2019. https://touchedbyahorse.com/gestalt-beyond-the-conscious-mind/

22. R. V. De Walker, Consciousness Is Pattern Recognition. Computer Science > Artificial Intelligence [Submitted on 4 May 2016 (v1), last revised 28 Jun 2016 (this version, v2)]. https://arxiv.org/abs/1605.03009

23. G. Eoyang, Patterns for Consciousness, November 2014. www.hsdinstitute.org/resources/patterns-for-consciousness-blog.html

24. Patterns of the Consciousness—An Introduction. www.renxueinternational.org/patterns-of-the-consciousness-an-introduction/

25. S. Pockett, Consciousness Is a Thing, Not a Process, Applied Sciences, 2017, 7(12), 1248. www.mdpi.com/2076-3417/7/12/1248

26. T. A. Carey, Consciousness as Control and Controlled Perception, Annals of Behavioral Science, 2018, 4(2), 3. https://behaviouralscience.imedpub.com/consciousness-as-control-and-controlled-perception-a-perspective.php?aid=23059

27. J. Shepherd, Conscious Control over Action, Mind & Language, 2015, 30(3), 320–344. https://doi.org/10.1111/mila.12082. https://onlinelibrary.wiley.com/doi/full/10.1111/mila.12082

28. D. F. Marks, I Am Conscious, Therefore, I Am: Imagery, Affect, Action, and a General Theory of Behavior, Brain Sciences, 2019, 9(5), 107. https://doi.org/10.3390/brainsci9050107. www.mdpi.com/2076-3425/9/5/107

29. K. R. Balapala, Conscious and Subconscious Processes of Human Mind. A Clandestine Entity Indeed! International Journal of Basic and Applied Medical Sciences, 2014, 4(1). www.cibtech.org/J-MEDICAL-SCIENCES/PUBLICATIONS/2014/Vol_4_No_1/JMS-63-077-KARTHEEK-CONSCIOUS-INDEED.pdf
30. Collective Consciousness. https://en.wikipedia.org/wiki/Collective_consciousness
31. P. S. Sapaty, Simulating Distributed and Global Consciousness Under Spatial Grasp Paradigm, Advances in Machine Learning & Artificial Intelligence, 2020, 1(1). www.opastpublishers.com/open-access-articles/simulating-distributed-and-global-consciousness-under-spatial-grasp-paradigm.pdf
32. P. S. Sapaty, Simulating Distributed and Global Consciousness under Spatial Grasp Paradigm, Mathematical Machines and Systems, 2020, 4. www.immsp.kiev.ua/publications/articles/2020/2020_4/Sapaty_04_20.pdf
33. P. Sapaty, Symbiosis of Real and Simulated Worlds Under Global Awareness and Consciousness. Abstract at: The Science of Consciousness Conference, TSC, 14–18 September 2020. https://eagle.sbs.arizona.edu/sc/report_poster_detail.php?abs=3696
34. K. Cherry, Consciousness in Psychology, 19 May 2023. www.verywellmind.com/what-is-consciousness-2795922
35. J. Sutton, Consciousness in Psychology: 8 Theories & Examples, 3 January 2021. https://positivepsychology.com/consciousness-psychology/
36. N. A. Conti, E. Keegan, F. Torrente, J. C. Stagnaro, Consciousness in Psychiatry, Vertex, 2008, 19(78), 19–28. www.researchgate.net/publication/5261624_Consciousness_in_psychiatry
37. Consciousness and Its Disorders. www.wikilectures.eu/w/Consciousness_and_its_disorders
38. J. M. Mecklin, The International Conscience, International Journal of Ethics, 1919, 29(3). www.jstor.org/stable/pdf/2377426.pdf
39. P. S. Sapaty, A Distributed Processing System, European Patent N 0389655, Publ. 10.11.93. European Patent Office.
40. P. S. Sapaty, Mobile Processing in Distributed and Open Environments. New York: John Wiley & Sons, 1999.
41. P. S. Sapaty, Ruling Distributed Dynamic Worlds. New York: John Wiley & Sons, 2005.
42. P. S. Sapaty, Managing Distributed Dynamic Systems with Spatial Grasp Technology. Springer, 2017.
43. P. S. Sapaty, Holistic Analysis and Management of Distributed Social Systems. Springer, 2018.
44. P. S. Sapaty, Complexity in International Security: A Holistic Spatial Approach. Emerald Publishing, 2019.
45. P. S. Sapaty, Symbiosis of Real and Simulated Worlds under Spatial Grasp Technology. Springer, 2021.

46. P. S. Sapaty, Spatial Grasp as a Model for Space-based Control and Management Systems. CRC Press, 2022.
47. P. S. Sapaty, The Spatial Grasp Model: Applications and Investigations of Distributed Dynamic Worlds. Emerald Publishing, 2023.
48. P. S. Sapaty, Relation of Spatial Grasp Paradigm to Higher Psychological and Mental Concepts, Acta Scientific Computer Sciences, 2022, 4(12). https://actascientific.com/ASCS/pdf/ASCS-04-0359.pdf
49. P. S. Sapaty, Seeing and Managing Distributed Worlds with Spatial Grasp Paradigm, Acta Scientific Computer Sciences, 2022, 4(12). https://actascientific.com/ASCS/pdf/ASCS-04-0365.pdf
50. P. S. Sapaty, Comprehending Distributed Worlds with the Spatial Grasp Paradigm, Mathematical Machines and Systems, 2022, 1. www.immsp.kiev.ua/publications/articles/2022/2022_1/01_22_Sapaty.pdf
51. P. S. Sapaty, Spatial Management of Air and Missile Defence Operations, Mathematical Machines and Systems, 2023, 1. www.immsp.kiev.ua/publications/articles/2023/2023_1/01_23_Sapaty.pdf
52. P. S. Sapaty, Providing Distributed System Integrity under Spatial Grasp Technology, Mathematical Machines and Systems, 2023, 2. www.immsp.kiev.ua/publications/articles/2023/2023_2/02_23_Sapaty.pdf
53. P. S. Sapaty, Providing Global Awareness in Distributed Dynamic Systems, International Relations and Diplomacy, 2023, 11(2), 87–100. https://doi.org/10.17265/2328-2134/2023.02.002. www.davidpublisher.com/Public/uploads/Contribute/6486c3d05a6cc.pdf
54. P. S. Sapaty, Simulating Distributed Consciousness with Spatial Grasp Model, Mathematical Machines and Systems, 2023, 3.
55. P. S. Sapaty, Managing Distributed Systems with Spatial Grasp Patterns, Mathematical Machines and Systems, 2023, 4.

7

MANAGING DISTRIBUTED SYSTEMS WITH SPATIAL GRASP PATTERNS

7.1 Introduction

Pattern is everything in the digital world. Patterns can be seen physically or observed mathematically by applying algorithms. A pattern, for example, can be as follows: an arrangement of lines or shapes, regularity in the world, human-made design, or abstract ideas, unvarying way of acting or doing, a model, plan, or diagram used as a guide, a standard way of moving, acting, and the like, a representation of a class or type, an example, sample, instance, or specimen, a distinctive style, model, or form, a combination of qualities, acts, or tendencies, and an original or model deserving of imitation. The aim of this chapter is to investigate and analyze the applicability of the developed Spatial Grasp Model and Technology, and especially its basic Spatial Grasp Language, for representation and implementation of different types of patterns, which can be used in simulation and management of a variety of distributed dynamic systems. These systems may cover such areas as education, economy, science, ecology, psychology, security, defense, international relations, space research, and many others. The rest of the paper is organized as follows. Section 7.2 reviews existing works on patterns, grouping them by the following categories: patterns definition and theory, different pattern types, pattern matching and recognition, and pattern languages. Section 7.3 reviews the main ideas of the Spatial Grasp Model and Technology and its Spatial Grasp Language, described in Chapters 2 and 3. Section 7.4 shows how practical patterns can be expressed under SGT, like creating regular patterns, patterns of concrete objects, and different patterns-based management solutions (including managing transport column, finding distributed zone coordinates, and spatial tracking of mobile

DOI: 10.1201/9781003425267-7

127

objects). It also gives network examples of distributed pattern recognition and matching solutions. Section 7.5 provides a summary of the investigated use of SGL, which can be represented as a real and universal pattern language. This summary is grouped for descriptive patterns, creative patterns, patterns as spatial processes, pattern recognition, self-matching patterns, combined patterns, cooperating and conflicting patterns, psychological patterns, and recursive patterns. Section 7.6 concludes the chapter with the obtained belief of applicability and effectiveness of SGL and SGT for expressing, representing, and processing patterns in different areas. References contain many discovered and analyzed pattern-based sources, as well as published papers and books on SGT and SGL.

7.2 Review of Existing Works on Patterns

After having been searched for, discovered, analyzed, compared, discussed, and classified, the existing pattern-based ideas, sources, and publications can be grouped as follows.

- **Pattern definition and theory**

  A pattern [1] is regularity in the world, in human-made design, or in abstract ideas. As such, the elements of a pattern repeat in a predictable manner. A geometric pattern is a kind of pattern formed of geometric shapes and typically repeated, like in wallpaper design. Any of the senses may directly observe patterns. Conversely, abstract patterns in science, mathematics, or language may be observable only by analysis.

  Pattern Theory: From Representation to Inference [2] provides a comprehensive and accessible overview of the modern challenges in signal, data, and pattern analysis in speech recognition, computational linguistics, image analysis, and computer vision. The book is aimed at graduate students in biomedical engineering, mathematics, computer science, and electrical engineering with a good background in mathematics and probability.

  Pattern Theory-Based Interpretation of Activities [3] presents a novel framework, based on Grenander's pattern theoretic concepts, for high-level interpretation of video activities. This framework allows us to elegantly integrate ontological constraints and machine learning classifiers in one formalism to construct high-level semantic interpretations that describe video activity.

Pattern Theory: A Unifying Perspective [4] introduced the term "pattern theory" as a name for a field of applied mathematics that gave a theoretical setting for a large number of related ideas, techniques, and results from fields such as computer vision, speech recognition, image and acoustic signal processing, pattern recognition, neural nets, and parts of artificial intelligence. Pattern theory contains the germs of a universal theory of thought itself, one which stands in opposition to the accepted analysis of thought in terms of logic.

Pattern theory [5] is a mathematical formalism to describe knowledge of the world as patterns. It differs from other approaches to artificial intelligence in that it does not begin by prescribing algorithms and machinery to recognize and classify patterns; rather, it prescribes a vocabulary to articulate and recast the pattern concepts in precise language. Pattern theory spans algebra and statistics, as well as local topological and global entropic properties.

* **Different pattern types**

Patterns of distributed systems are discussed in [6]. Distributed systems provide a particular challenge to program. Despite this, many organizations rely on a range of core distributed software handling data storage, messaging, system management, and compute capability. These systems face common problems, which they solve with similar solutions. The paper recognizes and develops these solutions as patterns helping to understand, communicate, and teach distributed system design.

Statistical descriptions of spatial patterns are discussed in [7]. Spatial statistics can be defined as a statistical description of spatial data and a spatial pattern or process. Spatial statistics allow a quantitative description along with indications of statistical significance in observational data on a pattern or a process operating in space. This quantitative and statistical description allows the exploration and modeling of spatial patterns and processes and their relationships with other spatial phenomena.

Recursive patterns are covered in [8]. An important goal of visualization technology is to support the exploration and analysis of very large amounts of data. This paper proposes a new visualization technique called a "recursive pattern," which has been developed for visualizing large amounts of multi-dimensional data. The technique is based on a generic recursive scheme that generalizes a wide range of pixel-oriented arrangements for displaying large data sets.

The Hidden Pattern: A Patternist Philosophy of Mind [9] presents a novel philosophy of mind, intended to form a coherent conceptual framework within which it is possible to understand the diverse aspects of mind and intelligence in a unified way. The central concept of the philosophy presented is the concept of "pattern": minds and the world they live in and co-create are viewed as patterned systems of patterns, evolving over time.

Workflow control-flow patterns are discussed in [10]. The Workflow Patterns Initiative aims at delineating fundamental requirements that arise during business process modeling and describes them in an imperative way. The first deliverable of this project was a set of 20 patterns describing the control-flow perspective of workflow systems. These patterns have been widely used by practitioners, vendors, and academics in the selection, design, and development of workflow systems.

Workflow patterns are also discussed in [11]. Requirements for workflow languages are indicated through workflow patterns. In this context, patterns address business requirements in an imperative workflow style expression. The paper describes a number of workflow patterns that can identify comprehensive workflow functionality. These patterns provide the basis for comparison of a number of commercially available workflow management systems.

- **Pattern matching and recognition**

Pattern matching is covered in [12]. In computer science, pattern matching is the act of checking a given sequence of tokens for the presence of the constituents of some pattern.

In contrast to pattern recognition, the match usually has to be exact: either it will or will not be a match. Uses of pattern matching include to output the locations of a pattern within a token sequence, to output some component of the matched pattern, and to substitute the matching pattern with some other token.

Fast graph pattern matching is discussed in [13]. Due to the rapid growth of internet technology and new scientific/technological advances, the number of applications that model data as graphs increases, because graphs have high expressive power to model complicated structures. The dominance of graphs in real-world applications asks for new graph data management so that users can access graph data effectively and efficiently. This paper studies a graph pattern matching problem over a large data graph.

Pattern matching in massive metadata graphs at scale is presented in [14]. Pattern matching in graphs, that is finding subgraphs that match a smaller template graph within the large background graph, is fundamental to graph analysis and serves a rich set of applications. Existing solutions have limited scalability, are difficult to parallelize, support only a limited set of search patterns, and/or focus on only a subset of real-world problems. This work explores avenues toward designing a scalable solution for subgraph pattern matching.

Pattern recognition [15] is the automated recognition of patterns and regularities in data. It has applications in statistical data analysis, signal processing, image analysis, information retrieval, bioinformatics, data compression, computer graphics, and machine learning. Pattern recognition has its origins in statistics and engineering; some modern approaches to pattern recognition include the use of machine learning.

Consciousness is pattern recognition, as discussed in [16]. This is a proof of the strong AI hypothesis, i.e. that machines can be conscious. It is a phenomenological proof that pattern-recognition and subjective consciousness are the same activity in different terms. Therefore, it proves that essential subjective processes of consciousness are computable and identifies significant traits and requirements of a conscious system.

Pattern recognition (psychology) is discussed in [17]. In psychology and cognitive neuroscience, pattern recognition describes a cognitive process that matches information from a stimulus with information retrieved from memory. Pattern recognition occurs when information from the environment is received and entered into short-term memory, causing automatic activation of a specific content of long-term memory.

- **Pattern languages**

Pattern language is discussed in [18]. The language description—the vocabulary—is a collection of named, described solutions to problems in a field of interest. These are called design patterns. So, for example, the language for architecture describes items like settlements, buildings, rooms, windows, and latches. Each solution includes syntax, a description that shows where the solution fits in a larger, more comprehensive or more abstract design.

Pattern language is also described in [19]. A pattern language is an organized and coherent set of patterns, each of which describes a problem and the core of a solution that can be used in many ways within a specific field of expertise. A pattern language can also be an attempt to express the deeper wisdom of what brings aliveness within a particular field of human endeavor, through a set of interconnected patterns.

A Pattern Language [20] creates a new language, what the authors call a pattern language derived from timeless entities called patterns. As they write in the introduction, all 253 patterns together form a language. *A Pattern Language* is structured as a network, where each pattern may have a statement referenced to another pattern by placing that pattern's number in brackets.

What is a pattern language is discussed in [21]. A pattern language is an attempt to express the deeper wisdom of what brings aliveness within a particular field of human endeavor, through a set of interconnected expressions arising from that wisdom. Aliveness is one placeholder term for "the quality that has no name": a sense of wholeness, spirit, or grace, that while of varying form, is precise and empirically verifiable.

In *Pattern Language: Towns, Buildings, Construction* [22], "patterns," the units of this language, are answers to design problems. More than 250 of the patterns in this pattern language are given: each consists of a problem statement, a discussion of the problem with an illustration, and a solution. Many of the patterns are archetypal, so deeply rooted in the nature of things that it seems likely that they will be a part of human nature and human action.

A pattern language for pattern language structure is covered in [23]. This paper aims to help the writers of pattern languages build better pattern languages. It focuses not on the esthetics of pattern languages, but on their structure: how patterns work together to build a system. The paper assumes that a pattern language is a designed system and, therefore, theory about system design and evolution underlies the language.

Growing a Pattern Language (for Security) [24] presents a pattern language containing all security patterns that have been published in various venues. It describes the mechanism of growing this pattern language: how to catalog the security patterns from books, papers, and pattern catalogs, how to classify the patterns to help developers find appropriate patterns, and how to identify and describe the relationships between patterns in the pattern language.

Pattern Languages as Media for the Creative Society [25] proposes new languages for basic skills in a creative society, where people create their own goods, tools, concepts, knowledge, and mechanisms with their own hands: the skills of learning, presentation, and collaboration. These languages are written as a pattern language, which is a way of describing the tacit practical knowledge.

In *Change Making Patterns. A Pattern Language for Fostering Social Entrepreneurship* [26], by conducting interviews with social entrepreneurs, a pattern language was created, named "Change Making Patterns." The objective of these patterns is to encourage more individuals to take own actions in making a better world with fewer social problems. The background of the patterns and how they can be applied for social entrepreneurial education are provided.

Pattern languages in interaction design are discussed in [27]. As individual patterns for interaction design have started to appear, the issue of structuring collections of patterns into pattern languages becomes relevant, from both a theoretical and a practical perspective. This paper investigates how pattern languages in interaction design can be structured in a meaningful and practical way. A top-down approach is taken where patterns for interaction design are organized hierarchically.

A pattern language for pattern writing is discussed in [28]. As the patterns community has accumulated experience in writing and reviewing patterns and pattern languages, the authors have begun to develop insight into pattern-writing techniques and approaches to be particularly effective at addressing certain recurring problems. This pattern language attempts to capture some of these "best practices" of pattern writing, both by describing them in pattern form and by demonstrating them in action.

7.3 Spatial Grasp Model and Technology Basics

This section reviews only key ideas of the basic model and technology that may useful to comprehend more quickly the material of this chapter, with technology details in Chapters 2 and 3 and more in [29–45]. Within Spatial Grasp Model and Technology, a high-level operational scenario is represented as an active self-evolving pattern rather than a traditional program. This pattern expressed in recursive Spatial Grasp Language, starting at any world point (or points), propagates, replicates, modifies, covers, and matches the distributed environment in parallel wavelike mode. This propagation also combines feedback echoing of the reached control states and obtained data, which may be remote, for making higher-level decisions, altogether providing holistic solutions unachievable by other models and systems. The SGL allows for expressing direct space presence and operations with unlimited parallelism. Its universal recursive organization with operational scenarios called *grasp* can be expressed just by a single string:

grasp → *constant* | *variable* | *rule* ({*grasp*,})

The SGL *rule* expresses certain action, control, description, or context accompanied with operands, which can themselves be any *grasp* too. Each SGL interpreter copy can handle and process multiple active SGL scenario code that is freely evolving and propagating in space and between the interpreters.

7.4 Patterns under SGT

Discusses different types of practical patterns expressed in SGL.

7.4.1 Creating Patterns

- **Regular patterns**

The two-step result of the following SGL scenario (first creating the full set of nodes in parallel, and then interconnecting them in parallel too) is shown in Figure 7.1.

```
nodal(Xmin = . . ., Ymin = . . .; Step = . . ., Number = . . .);
frontal(Xcurr), Link = type);
sequence(
   (Xcoord = array(Xmin, Step, Number);
    Ycoord = array(Ymin, Step, Number);
    parallel(split(Xcoord); Xcurr = VALUE);
    parallel(split(Ycoord); Ycurr = VALUE);
    create _ node(Xcurr, Ycurr)),
   (hop _ nodes(all);
    parallel(
       linkup(Link, node(shift _ X(Step)),
       linkup(Link, node(shift _ Y(-Step)),
       linkup(Link, node(shift _ X(Step));
       shift _ Y(-Step)))))
```

- **Patterns of concrete objects**

The results of the following SGL scenarios are shown in Figure 7.2.

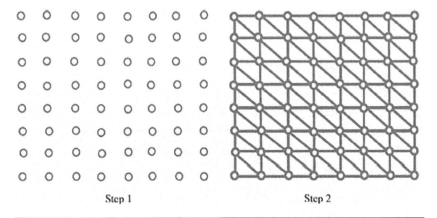

Step 1   Step 2

Figure 7.1   Creating a regular pattern.

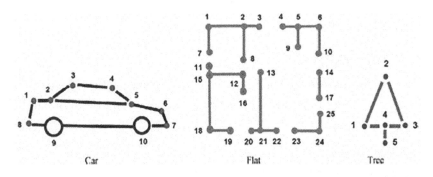

Car   Flat   Tree

Figure 7.2   Patterns of different objects.

Creating the car pattern:

```
frontal(N = . . ., L = blue, D = diameter);
create(N:2; L _ N:1; L _ N:8; L _ (N:9, D); L _ (N:10, D);
   L _ N:7; L _ N:6; L _ N:5; (L _ N:4; L _ N:3), stay);
   linkup(L _ N:2)
```

Creating the flat pattern:

```
frontal(N = . . ., L = grey);
create(
   (N:1; L _ N:7, (L _ N:2; L _ N:8, L _ N:3),
   (N:6; L _ N:10, (L _ N:5; L _ N:9, L _ N:4)),
   (N:18; L _ N:19, (L _ N:15; L _ N:11, (L _ N:12; L _ N:16)))),
```

```
(N:21: L _ N:20, L _ N:13, L _ N:22),
(N:24; L _ N:23, L _ N:25),
(N:14; L _ N:17))
```

Creating the tree pattern:

```
frontal(N = . . ., L = green);
create(N:5; L_N:4; L_N:1; L_N:2; L_N:3); linkup(L_N:4)
```

7.4.2 Pattern-Based Practical Solutions

- ### Managing transport column

Starting from the head vehicle, the SGL scenario propagates along the column and reduces gaps between vehicles, also leaving repetitive gap analyzing processes in each node, as in Figure 7.3.

```
frontal(Standard) = . . .;
hop _ vehicle(first);
repeat(
   free(nonequal(vehicle, first);
        repeat(if(distance(vehicle_ahead) > Standard,
                   reduce(distance(ahead), Standard),
                   stay)));
   hop _ vehicle(behind))
```

- ### Collecting zone coordinates

The following scenario, starting at some point near the distributed area, collects its border coordinates simultaneously in two directions, finally appending the obtained results to each other as the united sequence, as in Figure 7.4.

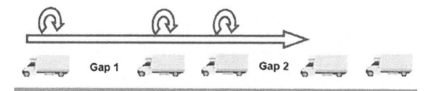

Figure 7.3   Correcting vehicle distances in their column.

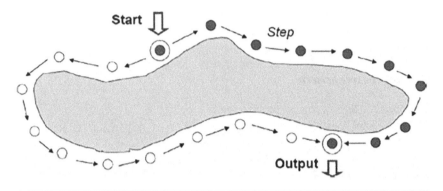

Figure 7.4   Collecting zone coordinates in two directions.

```
go(Start); frontal(Coord1, Step); nodal(Coord2);
parallel(
  repeat(append(Coord1, WHERE);
         if(seen(close, other),
            done(hop(other; output(append(Coord1,
            reverse(Coord2)));
         go(right, Step, Distance)),
    repeat(go(left, Step, Distance); append(Coord2,
           WHERE); if(seen(close, other), terminate)))
```

- **Tracking mobile objects**

The following self-evolving spatial scenario tracks and controls complex object propagating via a distributed network of radar stations, as in Figure 7.5.

```
hop(all_nodes); frontal(Object);
whirl(
  Object = search(aerial, new));
  visibility(Object) > threshold;
  repeat(
    loop(visibility(Object) > Threshold);
    max_destination(hop(all_neighbors);
    visibility(Object));
    visibility(Object) > Threshold)))
```

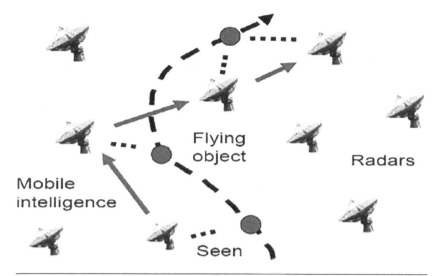

Figure 7.5 Distributed object tracking by a radar network.

7.4.3 Pattern Recognition and Matching

- **Pattern recognition**

The following scenarios recognize proper nodes and peculiar structures in a distributed network, as in Figure 7.6.

Finding all nodes having exactly five links to other nodes:

```
output(hop_nodes(all); count(hop_links(all)) == 5; NAME)
```

Answer: 49, 50, 69

Finding all cliques with the number of nodes equal to four.

```
hop _ nodes(all);
frontal(Clique = NAME, Number = 4);
repeat(
  hop _ links(all); notbelong(NAME, Clique);
  true(and_parallel(hop(link(any), nodes_all(Clique))));
  append(Clique, NAME);
  if(count(Clique) == Number, done(output(Clique))))
```

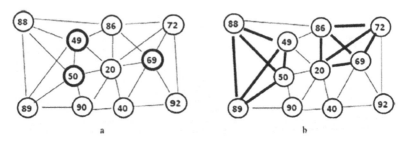

Figure 7.6 (a) Finding proper nodes; (b) discovering structures.

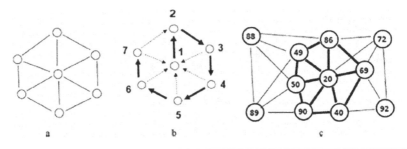

Figure 7.7 (a) Graph image; (b) its active template for finding exact match; (c) the match found in the network.

- **Pattern matching**

The following SGL scenario finds an exact match of the given image in a distributed network; see also Figure 7.7.

```
hop _ first _ nodes(all); COLOR = Match = NAME;
hop _ first _ links(all); Match = NAME;
repeat(5)(hop _ first _ links(all);
          true(hop _ links(any, node(Match[1])));
hop _ links(any, node(match[2]); output(Match)
```

One of the output results will be 20, 86, 69, 40, 90, 50, 49, with others with same elements but represented in different order. With elementary extension of the prior scenario, we may order receiving only unique sets of matched node names.

7.5 SGL as a Real Pattern Language

After detailed analyses and practical implementation and use of pattern-based solutions in many areas [29–44], SGL cannot be treated just as a networked set of specific patterns, like the existing pattern languages [18–28]. On the contrary, it reflects the universal paradigm capable to express and use any individual or general patterns and their systems, whether passive or active, and combines descriptive patterns with any centralized and distributed processes. A brief summary on this may be as follows, which can confirm that SGL can represent a real and very effective *pattern language* with practical applications in numerous areas.

• *Descriptive patterns*

Any pattern parts, their compositions, structures, with local or global parameters, can be naturally described in SGL and subsequently used for pattern recognition and matching by special processes.

• *Creative patterns*

Patterns describing composition and structures of different images, whether regular or arbitrary, can themselves be active parallel processes capable of creating or drawing such images autonomously in distributed spaces.

• *Patterns as spatial processes*

These can provide any investigation, control, management, and simulation of any systems, which may be terrestrial or celestial in nature. They can also express and simulate large distributed spatial processes like, say, the spread of global viruses and fighting them.

• *Pattern recognition*

This can be effectively organized in any physical, virtual, or combined system, where pattern recognition process relies on detailed or generalized pattern qualification and representation data, expressed in logical, numerical, or structural form.

• *Self-matching patterns*

Any graph-based pattern can be organized as active self-matching templates autonomously evolving and spreading in distributed spaces in wavelike parallel manner. They can return names, addresses, and/ or physical coordinates of the found elements and their structures and also influence the systems matched.

- *Combined patterns*

Any combinations of the aforementioned and following patterns, of any complexity, which can recognize, match, analyze, change, and control any distributed system can be effectively organized. And these patterns may virtually or physically migrate and fly over the covered systems in a controlled virus-like mode.

- *Cooperating and conflicting patterns*

Different self-powered patterns may compete or cooperate in the distributed systems and spaces, like representing collectives working on common problems or reflecting opposing units on a battlefield competing and destroying each other.

- *Psychological patterns*

As already shown and discussed in SGT-related publications (like [32, 33, 35] and others) the main gestalt psychology ideas, laws, and examples, based on mentally grasping the whole of concepts and events first, can be effectively represented and modeled with the use of spatial patterns.

- *Recursive patterns*

Patterns of any complexity can be effectively organized in SGL using its universal recursive structure, with any aforementioned patterns capable of including any other patterns, each of which can do the same and to unlimited depth.

7.6 Conclusions

We may conclude with a strong belief that SGL can be used as a real, very effective, and compact language for pattern representation and operations, truly named as *pattern language*. And SGT, in general, can and should contribute to the pattern theory and resultant technologies as a unique universal model treating the whole world, whether physical, virtual, or psychological and mental, as spatial patterns.

References

1. Pattern. https://en.wikipedia.org/wiki/Pattern

2. U. Grenander, M. Miller, Pattern Theory: From Representation to Inference (Oxford Studies in Modern European Culture). Oxford University Press, 2007. www.amazon.com/Pattern-Theory-Representation-Inference-European/dp/0199297061

3. F. D. M. de Souza, S. Sarkar, A. Srivastava, J. Su, Pattern Theory-Based Interpretation of Activities. 22nd International Conference on Pattern Recognition, 2014. https://projet.liris.cnrs.fr/imagine/pub/proceedings/ICPR-2014/data/5209a106.pdf

4. D. Mumford, Pattern Theory: A Unifying Perspective, Supported by NSF Grant DMS 91-21266 and by the Geometry Center, University of Minnesota, 28 September 1992. www.dam.brown.edu/people/mumford/vision/papers/1994c-96--PattThUnifyingPersp-NC.pdf

5. Pattern Theory. https://en.wikipedia.org/wiki/Pattern_theory

6. U. Joshi, Patterns of Distributed Systems, 7 September 2022. https://martinfowler.com/articles/patterns-of-distributed-systems/

7. T. Sankey, Statistical Descriptions of Spatial Patterns. In Shekhar, S., Xiong, H., Zhou, X. (Eds.), Encyclopedia of GIS. Cham: Springer, 2017. https://doi.org/10.1007/978-3-319-17885-1_1351. https://link.springer.com/referenceworkentry/10.1007/978-3-319-17885-1_1351

8. D. A. Keim, P. Kröger, M. Ankerst, Recursive Pattern: A Technique for Visualizing Very Large Amounts of Data. IEEE Xplore, Conference: Visualization, 1995. https://doi.org/10.1109/VISUAL.1995.485140. www.researchgate.net/publication/3618236_Recursive_pattern_A_technique_for_visualizing_very_large_amounts_of_data

9. B. Goertzel, The Hidden Pattern: A Patternist Philosophy of Mind, the Kurzweil Library + Collections, 27 December 2014. www.kurzweilai.net/the-hidden-pattern-a-patternist-philosophy-of-mind-2

10. N. Russell, A. H. M. ter Hofstede, W. M. P. van der Aalst, N. Mulyar, Workflow Control-Flow Patterns: A Revised View, 2006. www.workflowpatterns.com/documentation/documents/BPM-06-22.pdf

11. W. M. P. van der Aalst, A. H. M. der Hofstede, B. Kiepuszewski, A. P. Barros, Workflow Patterns, 2002. www.workflowpatterns.com/documentation/documents/wfs-pat-2002.pdf

12. Pattern Matching. https://en.wikipedia.org/wiki/Pattern_matching

13. J. Cheng, J. Xu Yu, B. Ding, P. S. Yu, H. Wang, Fast Graph Pattern Matching. www.microsoft.com/en-us/research/wp-content/uploads/2016/02/icde08gsearch.pdf

14. T. Reza, Pattern Matching in Massive Metadata Graphs at Scale, 2019. https://doi.org/10.14288/1.0387453. Corpus ID: 212778128. https://open.library.ubc.ca/soa/cIRcle/collections/ubctheses/24/items/1.0387453

15. Pattern Recognition. https://en.wikipedia.org/wiki/Pattern_recognition

16. R. Van De Walker, Consciousness Is Pattern Recognition, 2016. https://arxiv.org/abs/1605.03009

17. Pattern Recognition (Psychology). https://en.wikipedia.org/wiki/Pattern_recognition_(psychology)

18. Pattern Language. https://en.wikipedia.org/wiki/Pattern_language
19. Pattern Language. https://en.wikipedia.org/wiki/Pattern_language#:~: text=A%20pattern%20language%20is%20an,1977%20book%20A%20 Pattern%20Language
20. A Pattern Language. https://en.wikipedia.org/wiki/A_Pattern_Language
21. What Is a Pattern Language? https://groupworksdeck.org/pattern-language
22. C. Alexander, S. Ishikawa, M. Silverstein, et al., A Pattern Language: Towns, Buildings, Construction (Center for Environmental Structure Series). Oxford University Press, 1977. www.amazon.com/Pattern-Language-Buildings-Construction-Environmental/dp/0195019199
23. T. Winn, P. Calder, A Pattern Language for Pattern Language Structure. Appeared at Third Asian Pacific Conference on Pattern Languages of Programs (KoalaPLoP 2002), January 2003. www.researchgate.net/ publication/228944468_A_pattern_language_for_pattern_language_ structure
24. M. Hafiz, P. Adamczyk, R. Johnson, Growing a Pattern Language (for Security), Proceedings of the ACM International Symposium on New Ideas, New Paradigms, and Reflections on Programming and Software, October 2012. https://doi.org/10.1145/2384592.2384607. www.researchgate.net/publication/262211609_Growing_a_pattern_ language_for_security
25. T. Iba, Pattern Languages as Media for the Creative Society, Journal of Information Processing and Management, 2013, 55(12). https:// doi.org/10.1241/johokanri.55.865. www.researchgate.net/publication/ 255484746_Pattern_Languages_as_Media_for_the_Creative_Society
26. T. Iba, Change Making Patterns. A Pattern Language for Fostering Social Entrepreneurship. https://citeseerx.ist.psu.edu/viewdoc/download? doi=10.1.1.677.5339&rep=rep1&type=pdf
27. M. Van Welie, G. van der Veer, Pattern Languages in Interaction Design: Structure and Organization, October 2011. www.researchgate.net/ publication/228881522_Pattern_languages_in_interaction_design_ Structure_and_organization
28. G. Meszaros, J. Doble, A Pattern Language for Pattern Writing, The Hillside Group. https://hillside.net/index.php/a-pattern-language-for-pattern-writing
29. P. S. Sapaty, A Distributed Processing System, European Patent N 0389655, Publ. 10.11.93. European Patent Office.
30. P. S. Sapaty, Mobile Processing in Distributed and Open Environments. New York: John Wiley & Sons, 1999.
31. P. S. Sapaty, Ruling Distributed Dynamic Worlds. New York: John Wiley & Sons, 2005.
32. P. S. Sapaty, Managing Distributed Dynamic Systems with Spatial Grasp Technology. Springer, 2017.
33. P. S. Sapaty, Holistic Analysis and Management of Distributed Social Systems. Springer, 2018.

34. P. S. Sapaty, Complexity in International Security: A Holistic Spatial Approach. Emerald Publishing, 2019.
35. P. S. Sapaty, Symbiosis of Real and Simulated Worlds under Spatial Grasp Technology. Springer, 2021.
36. P. S. Sapaty, Spatial Grasp as a Model for Space-based Control and Management Systems. CRC Press, 2022.
37. P. S. Sapaty, The Spatial Grasp Model: Applications and Investigations of Distributed Dynamic Worlds. Emerald Publishing, 2023.
38. P. S. Sapaty, Relation of Spatial Grasp Paradigm to Higher Psychological and Mental Concepts, Acta Scientific Computer Sciences, 2022, 4(12). https://actascientific.com/ASCS/pdf/ASCS-04-0359.pdf
39. P. S. Sapaty, Seeing and Managing Distributed Worlds with Spatial Grasp Paradigm, Acta Scientific Computer Sciences, 2022, 4(12). https://actascientific.com/ASCS/pdf/ASCS-04-0365.pdf
40. P. S. Sapaty, Comprehending Distributed Worlds with the Spatial Grasp Paradigm, Mathematical Machines and Systems, 2022, 1. www.immsp.kiev.ua/publications/articles/2022/2022_1/01_22_Sapaty.pdf
41. P. S. Sapaty, Spatial Management of Air and Missile Defence Operations, Mathematical Machines and Systems, 2023, 1. www.immsp.kiev.ua/publications/articles/2023/2023_1/01_23_Sapaty.pdf
42. P. S. Sapaty, Providing Distributed System Integrity under Spatial Grasp Technology, Mathematical Machines and Systems, 2023, 2. www.immsp.kiev.ua/publications/articles/2023/2023_2/02_23_Sapaty.pdf
43. P. S. Sapaty, Providing Global Awareness in Distributed Dynamic Systems, International Relations and Diplomacy, 2023, 11(2), 87–100. https://doi.org/10.17265/2328-2134/2023.02.002. www.davidpublisher.com/Public/uploads/Contribute/6486c3d05a6cc.pdf
44. P. S. Sapaty, Simulating Distributed Consciousness with Spatial Grasp Model, Mathematical Machines and Systems, 2023, 3.
45. P. S. Sapaty, Managing Distributed Systems with Spatial Grasp Patterns, Mathematical Machines and Systems, 2023, 4.

8
CONCLUSIONS

8.1 Introduction

The ideas of this book originate from the mobile WAVE approach [1–10] that allowed us, more than a half century ago, to implement citywide heterogeneous computer networks and solve distributed problems on them, well before the internet. The invented paradigm, which evolved into Spatial Grasp Technology, resulted in a European patent [11] and eight John Wiley, Springer, Emerald, and Taylor & Francis books [12–19] oriented on concrete applications in graph and network theory, defense and social systems, crisis management, simulation of global viruses, gestalt theory, collective robotics, space research, and many others. The obtained solutions often exhibited high system qualities like global integrity, distributed awareness, and even a sort of consciousness. The current book has chosen these important characteristics, that is, *integrity*, *awareness*, and *consciousness*, as primary research objectives, together with the theory of *patterns* covering them all.

The rest of this concluding chapter is organized as follows. Section 8.2 outlines the main issues of the Spatial Grasp Model and Technology, enabling us to achieve the results presented in the book in the areas of system integrity, awareness, consciousness, and pattern usage. Section 8.3 informs about the main results of the book while providing excerpts from different chapters on system self-recovery, distributed awareness, global societal consciousness, and pattern matching. It integrates the four research areas into a holistic qualitative system to be used as a whole for the investigation and creation of intelligent distributed systems. Section 8.4 mentions further research directions, which may include *spatial awareness*, *pattern recognition in psychology*, and practical use of the controversial idea that *consciousness may exist outside of the brain*. It also emphasizes the importance of psychology and psychiatry for resolving international

DOI: 10.1201/9781003425267-8

conflicts, mentioning the known correspondence on that matter between Albert Einstein and Sigmund Freud. Section 8.5 concludes the chapter by summarizing the book's results in general, addressing technology implementation issues, and discussing market orientation. References point at numerous existing ideas and publications in the book's research areas, which were studied in detail and properly classified in the book.

8.2 Features of the Used Spatial Grasp Model and Technology

This section reviews the key ideas of the model and technology on which this book is based. It provides details on the paradigm in Chapters 2 and 3, as well as in previous books [12–19] and additional resources available on the internet by searching for "spatial grasp."

Within Spatial Grasp Model and Technology (SGT), a high-level operational scenario is represented as an *active self-evolving pattern* rather than a traditional program. This pattern expressed in recursive Spatial Grasp Language (SGL), starting at any world point (or points), propagates, replicates, modifies, covers, and matches the distributed environment in parallel wavelike mode. This propagation also combines feedback echoing of the reached control states and obtained data, which may be remote, for making higher-level decisions, altogether providing holistic spatial solutions unachievable by other models and systems (a symbolic paradigm expression is in Figure 8.1).

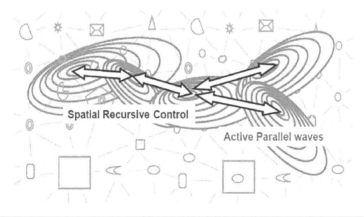

Figure 8.1 World coverage, matching, and control with the Spatial Grasp Model.

SGL allows for direct space presence and operations with unlimited mobility and parallelism. Its universal recursive organization with operational scenarios called *grasp* can be expressed by just a single string:

$$grasp \quad \rightarrow \quad constant \mid variable \mid rule \; (\{grasp,\})$$

where different types of *constants* and *variables* can appear and be located anywhere, and moreover, can propagate in physical and virtual spaces. The SGL *rule* expresses certain action, control, description, or context accompanied with operands, which can themselves be any *grasp*. The language is effectively processed by distributed networks with embedded SGL interpreters, where each interpreter copy can support multiple SGL scenario codes that are self-evolving and self-propagating in space and between the interpreters.

8.3 Extended Book Results

The book has provided the review and classification of numerous publications in the areas of integrity [20–31], awareness [32–46], and consciousness [47–84], also on pattern theory and practice [85–112]. It has then discussed and experimentally showed how to express their main features in SGL with orientation on full coverage and support of these areas by SGT. The results obtained are useful for the creation of advanced civil, defense, and security systems of any terrestrial or celestial nature that can efficiently operate even in unpredictable and critical situations.

8.3.1 Excerpts from Results in Different Chapters

Some excerpts from SGT- and SGL-based results from the book's various chapters are copied in Figure 8.2, including (a) how a total self-recovery of a distributed system can be organized if at least one of its nodes remains alive, as in Chapter 4; (b) how to provide full distributed awareness of an arbitrary large system about its basic components, their connections, structures of any complexity and any level, and any global assessments from any and to any system component, as in Chapter 5; (c) how to supply very large distributed

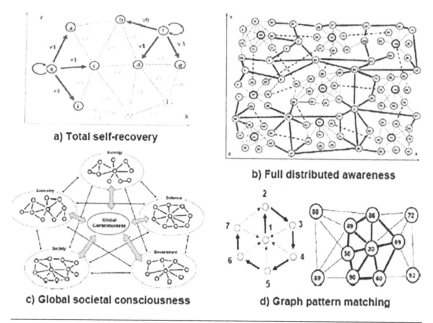

a) Total self-recovery

b) Full distributed awareness

c) Global societal consciousness

d) Graph pattern matching

Figure 8.2   Some excerpts from the book's results.

systems, including those of whole countries, with a sort of global consciousness, which by the resultant global assessments, feelings, and judgments can orient their operation and further developments in the most progressive ways, as in Chapter 6; and (d) how to organize parallel pattern matching of any graph-based images with arbitrary large, complex, and distributed system structures, with SGL proving to be a real and very efficient pattern language, as in Chapter 7.

8.3.2 Integrating Researched Areas into a Holistic Management System

These researched areas are forming altogether a very important and integral conceptual area, symbolically shown in Figure 8.3, which may be worth further investigation as a united whole for advanced intelligent systems.

Additionally, we mention next some (from numerous) existing publications that show and discuss direct links between these four areas (not mentioned in Chapters 4 to 7), which may be useful for further theoretical and practical investigations of this united *integrity-awareness-consciousness-patterns* area.

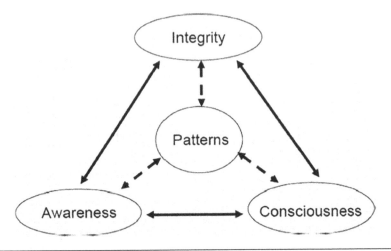

Figure 8.3 Integrating research and results obtained in different areas within a holistic system.

- **Between integrity and awareness**

Integrity Awareness Initiative [113] is to raise staff members' level of awareness of the core values of integrity, professionalism, and respect for diversity and to provide guidance about appropriate actions and people.

- **Between integrity and consciousness**

What Is Conscious Integrity? [114]. You have a unique set of values, desires, ethics, and commitments. How well do your life and your actions reflect these parts of your being? In this way, integrity is the link that binds your actions to your values, desires, ethics, and the world.

- **Between awareness and consciousness**

Are Consciousness and Awareness the Same? [115]. According to psychophysiologist Stephen LaBerge, consciousness is awareness plus mind and the structure of the individual brain. Consciousness does have to do with the brain, but it's not awareness.

- **Between patterns and integrity**

A Pattern of Integrity [116]. Patterns are used extensively in all aspects of life and living. Aircraft flight patterns are used to ensure that passengers are safe. This principle of patterns and integrity is even more applicable in our lives, both as professionals and as children of God.

- **Between patterns and awareness**

Patterns of Awareness [117]. Factors associated with group learning and development involve central control, loosening boundaries, challenging the obvious, psychological equilibrium and growth, respect for autonomy and participation, intellect and intuition, surrender of crystallized patterns, and faith.

- **Between patterns and consciousness**

Consciousness Is Pattern Recognition [118]. This is a proof of the strong AI hypothesis, i.e. that machines can be conscious. Therefore, it proves that the essential subjective processes of consciousness are computable and identifies significant traits and requirements of a conscious system.

8.4 More Research Planned

8.4.1 Directions That Need Further Investigation

Some of the directions for further investigation could be as follows.

Spatial awareness, as in Chapter 5, also [33], where *spatial reasoning* is how we understand how things (including ourselves) move and interact in relation to the physical space around them. SGT and SGL, based on spatial self-propagation, self-coverage, self-analysis, and self-evolution, need further investigations covering broader applications related to spatial awareness. For example, by extending the physical-virtual symbiosis discussed in [17] with psychology and psychiatry as the mental world, important results could be obtained from this tripled symbiosis for solving world problems [119, 120], and especially those linked with international relations.

Pattern recognition in psychology, as in Chapter 7, also [101], where pattern recognition describes a cognitive process that matches information from a stimulus with information retrieved from memory. In this direction, further investigations are needed, like expressing gestalt psychology laws in SGL started in [15], which emphasizes the ability of mind to grasp the whole of systems first with parts afterwards, and then analyzing the pattern theory in more detail. We began this in the current book, where SGL behaved as a real pattern language.

Consciousness outside of the brain, as in Chapter 6, also [63]. The consensus in neuroscience is that consciousness is an emergent property of the brain. But some believe that consciousness persists after death and *exists independently and outside of the brain*. SGT, as a spatially migrating parallel concept, can have different implementations. First, it can have its communicated scenarios embedded into the fabric of distributed systems with parts exchanging messages. Second, it can freely migrate as a distributed wavelike whole (like smog or flooding) with embedded full functionality throughout any environments, which can be outside or even far away from the systems managed. It can also be implemented as traditional computer viruses too, actually being itself the most powerful global virus in the history of computing and the internet (see also [1–10]), which can not only harm but rule and create too, with unlimited capabilities. Another implementation can use standard email for communications, with individually written SGL interpreters of the complexity needed (their basics are extremely simple) functioning as part of the user-owned software.

8.4.2 Linking Psychology and Psychiatry with International Problems

Returning to the *main world problems* discussed in Chapter 1, also [119, 120], we strongly believe that international peace should be on the forefront for solving many of them. *International peace*, as discussed in Chapter 6 and [84], is a question of a state of mind. "As a man thinks in his heart so is he" is as true of nations as of individuals. The *international conscience* is therefore the ultimate guarantee of international peace. It may also relate to *psychiatric consciousness*, as in Chapter 6 and [83], which is the ability to be aware of oneself in relation to the surrounding world; the ability to correctly interpret one's own experiences. If the ability to self-identify or experience experiences is "altered," then it can lead to "qualitative disorder," which on the international scale can result in conflicts and wars. The possible links between psychiatry and international affairs were discussed in [121], which mentioned the letter sent by Albert Einstein to Sigmund Freud (Figure 8.4) about the possibilities of having international peace.

The original of this letter in available at [122], in which Einstein wrote the following:

> Is it possible to control man's mental evolution so as to make him proof against the psychoses of hate and destructiveness? . . . I have so far been speaking only of wars between nations; what are known as international conflicts. But I am well aware that the aggressive instinct operates under other forms and in other circumstances. (I am thinking of civil wars, for instance, due in earlier days to religious zeal, but nowadays to social factors; or, again, the persecution of racial minorities).

There is also the original of very long, complicated, and not very adequate (by our assessment) answer of Freud [123], after which Einstein remained with his own opinion, as mentioned in [121].

We find this topic of linking psychology and psychiatry with international relations as extremely important and worth extended investigation, feeling that the developed recursive Spatial Grasp paradigm can contribute to this. With it, we can describe arbitrary complex psychological and psychiatric models of nations, using for their simulation the most advanced computer, communication, and information systems and networks. Such models can effectively

Figure 8.4 Communication between Einstein and Freud, 1932.

express both cooperation and competition and address potential conflicts between nations and countries. Their proper modifications with repeated simulations may lead to finding real strategies supporting world peace and prosperity. Plans for new books in this area are looming.

8.5 Conclusions

a. The results of investigation provided in this book confirm that SGT with its basic language SGL can effectively cover diverse systems problems, from their creation to analysis to modification to management, from traditional command and control to the highest levels of global integrity, overall awareness, and even distributed and global consciousness. As an extremely flexible mobile and self-evolving pattern based ideology and technology, it also covers the basics of the existing pattern theory so important for global world comprehension and operation in physical, virtual, and mental domains, including psychology and even psychiatry. The obtained results can also provide additional ground and practical examples for existing consciousness-related theories, on which common opinions have not been reached yet, due to their enormous diversity and complexity.

b. The described latest SGT version can be quickly implemented on any platform, even within traditional university environments, similar to the previous technology version's implementations and tests in different countries. The author will also be happy to provide any support needed for the new implementations, including cooperative preparation and writing of different application projects in SGL or its modified versions, which may be closer to the particular projects.

c. The current book is oriented to system scientists, application programmers, industry managers, defense and security commanders, and university students, especially those interested in advanced MSc and PhD projects on distributed system management, as well as philosophers, psychologists, and United Nations personnel.

References

1. A. T. Bondarenko, S. B. Mikhalevich, A. I. Nikitin, P. S. Sapaty, Software of BESM-6 Computer for Communication with Peripheral Computers via Telephone Channels. In Computer Software, Vol. 5. Kiev: Institute of Cybernetics Press, 1970.
2. P. S. Sapaty, A Method of Organization of an Intercomputer Dialogue in the Radial Computer Systems. In The Design of Software and Hardware for Automatic Control Systems. Kiev: Institute of Cybernetics Press, 1973.
3. P. S. Sapaty, Asynchronous Parallel Evolvent of Nonlinear and Control Algorithms. In Software for Control and Information Systems. Moscow House of Scientific and Technical Publicity, 1973.
4. P. S. Sapaty, On Possibilities of the Organization of a Direct Intercomputer Dialogue in ANALYTIC and FORTRAN Languages (Publ. No. 74–29). Kiev: Institute of Cybernetics Press, 1974.
5. P. S. Sapaty, A Method of Fast Dispatching for Parallel Execution of Tasks. In System Programming Languages and Methods of Their Implementation. Kiev: Institute of Cybernetics Press, 1974.
6. P. S. Sapaty, Solving Branching and Cycling Tasks on Multiprocessor Systems. Proceedings of the USSR Academy of Sciences: Technical Cybernetics, 1974, 1.
7. D. V. Karachenets, E. P. Pozdnjakov, V. N. Moroz, P. S. Sapaty, Questions of Using Dialogue in a Computer-Aided Analysis and Design of Complex Technological Systems. Proc. Republ. Conf. the Dialogue Tools for Solving Engineering Problems, Kiev, 1974.
8. A. T. Bondarenko, P. S. Sapaty, Algorithms of Distributing Independent Tasks on Parallel Devices, Proceedings of the USSR Academy of Sciences, Technical Cybernetics, 1975, 4.
9. P. S. Sapaty, Organization of Computational Processes in Distributed Heterogeneous Computer Networks, PhD Dissertation, Institute of Cybernetics, Kiev, 1976.
10. P. S. Sapaty, A Wave Language for Parallel Processing of Semantic Networks, Computing and Artificial Intelligence, 1986, 5(4), 289–314.
11. P. S. Sapaty, A Distributed Processing System, European Patent N 0389655, Publ. 10.11.93. European Patent Office.
12. P. S. Sapaty, Mobile Processing in Distributed and Open Environments. New York: John Wiley & Sons, 1999.
13. P. S. Sapaty, Ruling Distributed Dynamic Worlds. New York: John Wiley & Sons, 2005.
14. P. S. Sapaty, Managing Distributed Dynamic Systems with Spatial Grasp Technology. Springer, 2017.
15. P. S. Sapaty, Holistic Analysis and Management of Distributed Social Systems. Springer, 2018.
16. P. S. Sapaty, Complexity in International Security: A Holistic Spatial Approach. Emerald Publishing, 2019.

17. P. S. Sapaty, Symbiosis of Real and Simulated Worlds under Spatial Grasp Technology. Springer, 2021.

18. P. S. Sapaty, Spatial Grasp as a Model for Space-based Control and Management Systems. CRC Press, 2022.

19. P. S. Sapaty, The Spatial Grasp Model: Applications and Investigations of Distributed Dynamic Worlds. Emerald Publishing, 2023.

20. M. Mittal, R. Sangani, K. Srivastava, Testing Data Integrity in Distributed Systems, Procedia Computer Science, 2015, 45, 446–452. www.sciencedirect.com/science/article/pii/S1877050915003130

21. T. Rauter, Integrity of Distributed Control Systems. Student Forum of the 46th Annual IEEE/IFIP International Conference on Dependable Systems and Networks (hal-01318372), Toulouse, June 2016. https://hal. science/hal-01318372/file/DSN-Student-Forum_%237_Integrity-of-Distributed-Control-Systems.pdf

22. G. Sivanandham, J. M. Gnanasekar, Data Integrity and Recovery Management in Cloud Systems. Proceedings of the Fourth International Conference on Inventive Systems and Control (ICISC 2020) DVD Part Number: CFP20J06-DVD. www.researchgate.net/publication/343751352_Data_Integrity_and_Recovery_Management_in_Cloud_Systems

23. G. K. Sodhi, Recovery and Security in Distributed System, International Journal of Advanced Research in Computer and Communication Engineering, 2015, 4(12). www.ijarcce.com/upload/2015/december-15/IJARCCE%20105.pdf

24. X. Sun, J. Chen, H. Zhao, W. Zhang, Y. Zhang, Sequential Disaster Recovery Strategy for Resilient Distribution Network Based on Cyber–Physical Collaborative Optimization, IEEE Transactions on Smart Grid, 2023, 14(2), 1173–1187. https://doi.org/10.1109/TSG.2022.3198696. https://ieeexplore.ieee.org/document/9857641

25. V. Popa-Simil, H. Poston, Mrs. Thomas, L. Popa-Simil, Self-Recovery of a Distributed System After a Large Disruption, New Mexico Supercomputing Challenge, Final Report, 1 April 2012. www. supercomputingchallenge.org/11-12/finalreports/15.pdf

26. Y. Watanabe, S. Sato, Y. Ishida, An Approach for Self-repair in Distributed System Using Immunity-Based Diagnostic Mobile Agents. In Negoita, M. G. et al. (Eds.), KES 2004, LNAI 3214. Berlin and Heidelberg: Springer-Verlag, 2004, pp. 504–510. https://link.springer. com/chapter/10.1007/978-3-540-30133-2_66

27. A. M. Farley, A. Proskurowski, Minimum Self-Repairing Graphs, Graphs and Combinatorics, 1997, 13, 345–351. https://doi.org/10.1007/BF03353012. https://link.springer.com/article/10.1007/BF03353012

28. I. B. Hafaiedh, M. B. Slimane, A Distributed Formal-Based Model for Self-Healing Behaviors in Autonomous Systems: From Failure Detection to Self-Recovery, The Journal of Supercomputing, 2022, 78, 18725–18753. https://link.springer.com/article/10.1007/s11227-022-04614-0

29. J. Nikolic, N. Jubatyrov, E. Pournaras, Self-Healing Dilemmas in Distributed Systems: Fault Correction vs. Fault Tolerance, Journal of Latex Class Files, 2021, X(X). https://arxiv.org/pdf/2007.05261.pdf

30. W. Quattrociocchi, G. Caldarelli, A. Scala, Self-Healing Networks: Redundancy and Structure, PLoS One, 2014, 9(2), e87986. file:///C:/Users/user/Downloads/2014-02Self-healingnetworksredundancyand structure.pdf

31. A. Rodríguez, J. Gómez, A. Diaconescu, A Decentralised Self-Healing Approach for Network Topology Maintenance, Autonomous Agents and Multi-Agent Systems, 2021, 35, Article Number 6. https://link.springer. com/article/10.1007/s10458-020-09486-3

32. Awareness. https://en.wikipedia.org/wiki/Awareness

33. What Is Spatial Awareness? https://numeracyforallab.ca/what-we-learned/developing-spatial-awareness/

34. Total Information Awareness. https://en.wikipedia.org/wiki/Total_Information_Awareness

35. R. Mohanan, What Are Distributed Systems? Architecture Types, Key Components, and Examples, 12 January 2022. www.spiceworks.com/tech/cloud/articles/what-is-distributed-computing/

36. P. M. Salmon, K. L. Plant, Distributed Situation Awareness: From Awareness in Individuals and Teams to the Awareness of Technologies, Sociotechnical Systems, and Societies, Applied Ergonomics, 2022, 98, 103599. www.sciencedirect.com/science/article/abs/pii/S00036870 21002465

37. N. A. Stanton, Distributed Situation Awareness, Contemporary Ergonomics and Human Factors. In Charles, R., Wilkinson, J. (Eds.), CIEHF, 2016. https://publications.ergonomics.org.uk/uploads/Distributed-Situation-Awareness.pdf

38. M. M. Chatzimichailidou, A. Protopapas, I. M. Dokas, Seven Issues on Distributed Situation Awareness Measurement in Complex Sociotechnical Systems. In Boulanger, F., Krob, D., Morel, G., Roussel, J. C. (Eds.), Complex Systems Design & Management. Cham: Springer, 2015. https://doi.org/10.1007/978-3-319-11617-4_8. https://link.springer.com/chapter/10.1007/978-3-319-11617-4_8

39. E. Sultanov, E. Weber, Real World Awareness in Distributed Organizations: A View on Informal Processes, 2011. www.researchgate.net/publication/234720130_Real_World_Awareness_in_Distributed_Organizations_A_View_on_Informal_Processes

40. P. M. Salmon, N. A. Stanton, D. P. Jenkins, Distributed Situation Awareness Theory, Measurement and Application to Teamwork, By Copyright 2009, Published March 31, 2017 by CRC Press. www.routledge.com/Distributed-Situation-Awareness-Theory-Measurement-and-Application-to/Salmon-Stanton-Jenkins/p/book/9781138 073852

41. M. M. Chatzimichailidou, R. Freund, I. Dokas, Distributed Situation Awareness as a "Middleware" Between the New Economic Sociology and Embedded Open Innovation. 6th International Conference on Mass Customization and Personalization in Central Europe (MCP-CE 2014). https://mcp-ce.org/wp-content/uploads/proceedings/2014/6_chatzimichailidou.pdf

42. J. S. Preden, J. Helander, Context Awareness in Distributed Computing Systems, Annales Universitatis Scientiarum Budapestinensis de Rolando Eötvös Nominatae.Sectio computatorica, 2009, 31, 57–73. www.researchgate.net/publication/255564252_Context_Awareness_in_Distributed_Computing_Systems

43. S. Jones, E. Milner, M. Sooriyabandara, S. Hauert, Distributed Situational Awareness in Robot Swarms, Advanced Intelligent Systems, 2020, 2. https://onlinelibrary.wiley.com/doi/10.1002/aisy.202000110

44. S. K. Gan, Z. Xu, S. Sukkarieh, Distributed Situational Awareness and Control, UAS Multi-Vehicle Cooperation and Coordination, 13 June 2016. https://onlinelibrary.wiley.com/doi/full/10.1002/9780470686652.eae1133

45. L. Ge, Y. Li, J. Yan, Y. Sun, Smart Distribution Network Situation Awareness for High-Quality Operation and Maintenance: A Brief Review, Energies, 2022, 15(3), 828. https://doi.org/10.3390/en15030828

46. J. Tanveer, A. Haider, R. Ali, A. Kim, An Overview of Reinforcement Learning Algorithms for Handover Management in 5G Ultra-Dense Small Cell Networks, Applied Sciences, 2022, 12(1), 426. https://doi.org/10.3390/app12010426 www.mdpi.com/2076-3417/12/1/426

47. Consciousness. https://en.wikipedia.org/wiki/Consciousness

48. Hard Problem of Consciousness. https://en.wikipedia.org/wiki/Hard_problem_of_consciousness

49. M. Graziano, A New Theory Explains How Consciousness Evolved, The Atlantic, 6 June 2016. www.theatlantic.com/science/archive/2016/06/how-consciousness-evolved/485558/

50. K. Schultz, Consciousness: Definition, Examples, & Theory. The Berkeley Well-Being Institute, LLC, 2023. www.berkeleywellbeing.com/consciousness.html

51. A. Pereira Jr., The Projective Theory of Consciousness: From Neuroscience to Philosophical Psychology, Trans/Form/Ação, Marília, 2018, 41, 199–232, Edição Especial. www.scielo.br/j/trans/a/5xcwgRK9wtfkf4Wm48FKGfv/?format=pdf&lang=en

52. Models of Consciousness. https://en.wikipedia.org/wiki/Models_of_consciousness

53. A. Seth, Models of Consciousness, Scholarpedia, 2007, 2(1), 1328. www.scholarpedia.org/article/Models_of_consciousness

54. D. Rudrauf, D. Bennequin, I. Granic, G. Landini, K. Friston, K. Williford, A Mathematical Model of Embodied Consciousness, Journal of Theoretical Biology, 2017, 428, 106–131. www.sciencedirect.com/science/article/abs/pii/S0022519317302540

55. Artificial Consciousness. https://en.wikipedia.org/wiki/Artificial_consciousness

56. P. O. Haikonen, Consciousness and Robot Sentience (2nd Edition, Machine Consciousness). World Scientific, 2019. www.amazon.com/Consciousness-Robot-Sentience-2nd-Machine/dp/9811205043

57. A. Sloman, R. Chrisley, Virtual Machines and Consciousness, Journal of Consciousness Studies, 2003, 10(4–5). www.cs.bham.ac.uk/research/projects/cogaff/sloman-chrisley-jcs03.pdf

58. P. Krauss, A. Maier, Will We Ever Have Conscious Machines? Frontiers in Computational Neuroscience, 2020, 14. https://doi.org/10.3389/fncom.2020.556544. www.frontiersin.org/articles/10.3389/fncom.2020.556544/full

59. P. Sjöstedt-H, Consciousness and Higher Spatial Dimensions, 14 April 2022. https://iai.tv/articles/consciousness-and-higher-spatial-dimensions-auid-2107

60. T. Das, Brain Waves Create Consciousness, International Journal of Development Research, 2018, 8(6), 20910–20912. www.journalijdr.com/brain-waves-create-consciousness

61. R. Pepperell, Consciousness as a Physical Process Caused by the Organization of Energy in the Brain, Sec. Consciousness Research, 2018, 9. www.frontiersin.org/articles/10.3389/fpsyg.2018.02091/full

62. B. Bower, Spreading Consciousness, Awareness Goes Global in the Brain, Science News, 15 October 2002. www.sciencenews.org/article/spreading-consciousness

63. C. N. Lazarus, Can Consciousness Exist Outside of the Brain? The Brain May Not Create Consciousness But "Filter" It, Psychology Today, 26 June 2019. www.psychologytoday.com/intl/blog/think-well/201906/can-consciousness-exist-outside-the-brain

64. H. Wahbeh, D. Radin, C. Cannard, A. Delorme, What If Consciousness Is Not an Emergent Property of the Brain? Observational and Empirical Challenges to Materialistic Models, Frontiers in Psychology, 2022, 13. www.frontiersin.org/articles/10.3389/fpsyg.2022.955594/full

65. R. Manzotti, The Spread Mind: Why Consciousness and the World Are One. OR Books, 2018. www.amazon.com/Spread-Mind-Why-Consciousness-World/dp/1944869492

66. J. Smallwood, J. W. Schooler, The Science of Mind Wandering: Empirically Navigating the Stream of Consciousness, Annual Review of Psychology, 2015, 66, 487–518. https://pubmed.ncbi.nlm.nih.gov/25293689/

67. M. Pearce, Gestalt: Beyond the Conscious Mind, 2 May 2019. https://touchedbyahorse.com/gestalt-beyond-the-conscious-mind/

68. R. V. De Walker, Consciousness Is Pattern Recognition. Computer Science > Artificial Intelligence [Submitted on 4 May 2016 (v1), last revised 28 Jun 2016 (this version, v2)]. https://arxiv.org/abs/1605.03009

69. G. Eoyang, Patterns for Consciousness, November 2014. www.hsdinstitute.org/resources/patterns-for-consciousness-blog.html

70. Patterns of the Consciousness—An Introduction. www.renxueinternational. org/patterns-of-the-consciousness-an-introduction/

71. S. Pockett, Consciousness Is a Thing, Not a Process, Applied Sciences, 2017, 7(12), 1248. www.mdpi.com/2076-3417/7/12/1248

72. T. A. Carey, Consciousness as Control and Controlled Perception, Annals of Behavioral Science, 2018, 4(2), 3. https://behaviouralscience. imedpub.com/consciousness-as-control-and-controlled-perception-a-perspective.php?aid=23059

73. J. Shepherd, Conscious Control over Action, Mind & Language, 2015, 30(3), 320–344. https://doi.org/10.1111/mila.12082. https://onlinelibrary. wiley.com/doi/full/10.1111/mila.12082

74. D. F. Marks, I Am Conscious, Therefore, I Am: Imagery, Affect, Action, and a General Theory of Behavior, Brain Sciences, 2019, 9(5), 107. https:// doi.org/10.3390/brainsci9050107. www.mdpi.com/2076-3425/9/5/107

75. K. R. Balapala, Conscious and Subconscious Processes of Human Mind. A Clandestine Entity Indeed! International Journal of Basic and Applied Medical Sciences, 2014, 4(1). www.cibtech.org/J-MEDICAL-SCIENCES/PUBLICATIONS/2014/Vol_4_No_1/JMS-63-077-KARTHEEK-CONSCIOUS-INDEED.pdf

76. Collective Consciousness. https://en.wikipedia.org/wiki/Collective_ consciousness

77. P. S. Sapaty, Simulating Distributed and Global Consciousness Under Spatial Grasp Paradigm, Advances in Machine Learning & Artificial Intelligence, 2020, 1(1). www.opastpublishers.com/open-access-articles/ simulating-distributed-and-global-consciousness-under-spatial-grasp-paradigm.pdf

78. P. S. Sapaty, Simulating Distributed and Global Consciousness under Spatial Grasp Paradigm, Mathematical Machines and Systems, 2020, 4. www.immsp.kiev.ua/publications/articles/2020/2020_4/Sapaty_04_ 20.pdf

79. P. Sapaty, Symbiosis of Real and Simulated Worlds Under Global Awareness and Consciousness. Abstract at: The Science of Consciousness Conference, TSC, 14–18 September 2020. https://eagle.sbs.arizona.edu/ sc/report_poster_detail.php?abs=3696

80. K. Cherry, Consciousness in Psychology, 19 May 2023. www.verywellmind. com/what-is-consciousness-2795922

81. J. Sutton, Consciousness in Psychology: 8 Theories & Examples, 3 January 2021. https://positivepsychology.com/consciousness-psychology/

82. N. A. Conti, E. Keegan, F. Torrente, J. C. Stagnaro, Consciousness in Psychiatry, Vertex, 2008, 19(78), 19–28. www.researchgate.net/ publication/5261624_Consciousness_in_psychiatry

83. Consciousness and Its Disorders. www.wikilectures.eu/w/Consciousness_ and_its_disorders

84. J. M. Mecklin, The International Conscience, International Journal of Ethics, 1919, 29(3). www.jstor.org/stable/pdf/2377426.pdf

85. Pattern. https://en.wikipedia.org/wiki/Pattern

86. U. Grenander, M. Miller, Pattern Theory: From Representation to Inference (Oxford Studies in Modern European Culture). Oxford University Press, 2007. www.amazon.com/Pattern-Theory-Representation-Inference-European/dp/0199297061

87. D. Mumford, Pattern Theory: A Unifying Perspective, Supported by NSF Grant DMS 91-21266 and by the Geometry Center, University of Minnesota, 28 September 1992. www.dam.brown.edu/people/mumford/vision/papers/1994c-96--PattThUnifyingPersp-NC.pdf

88. F. D. M. de Souza, S. Sarkar, A. Srivastava, J. Su, Pattern Theory-Based Interpretation of Activities. 22nd International Conference on Pattern Recognition, 2014. https://projet.liris.cnrs.fr/imagine/pub/proceedings/ICPR-2014/data/5209a106.pdf

89. Pattern Theory. https://en.wikipedia.org/wiki/Pattern_theory

90. U. Joshi, Patterns of Distributed Systems, 7 September 2022. https://martinfowler.com/articles/patterns-of-distributed-systems/

91. T. Sankey, Statistical Descriptions of Spatial Patterns. In Shekhar, S., Xiong, H., Zhou, X. (Eds.), Encyclopedia of GIS. Cham: Springer, 2017. https://doi.org/10.1007/978-3-319-17885-1_1351. https://link.springer.com/referenceworkentry/10.1007/978-3-319-17885-1_1351

92. D. A. Keim, P. Kröger, M. Ankerst, Recursive Pattern: A Technique for Visualizing Very Large Amounts of Data. IEEE Xplore, Conference: Visualization, 1995. https://doi.org/10.1109/VISUAL.1995.485140. www.researchgate.net/publication/3618236_Recursive_pattern_A_technique_for_visualizing_very_large_amounts_of_data

93. B. Goertzel, The Hidden Pattern: A Patternist Philosophy of Mind, the Kurzweil Library + Collections, 27 December 2014. www.kurzweilai.net/the-hidden-pattern-a-patternist-philosophy-of-mind-2

94. N. Russell, A. H. M. ter Hofstede, W. M. P. van der Aalst, N. Mulyar, Workflow Control-Flow Patterns: A Revised View, 2006. www.workflowpatterns.com/documentation/documents/BPM-06-22.pdf

95. W. M. P. van der Aalst, A. H. M. der Hofstede, B. Kiepuszewski, A. P. Barros, Workflow Patterns, 2002. www.workflowpatterns.com/documentation/documents/wfs-pat-2002.pdf

96. Pattern Matching. https://en.wikipedia.org/wiki/Pattern_matching

97. J. Cheng, J. Xu Yu, B. Ding, P. S. Yu, H. Wang, Fast Graph Pattern Matching. www.microsoft.com/en-us/research/wp-content/uploads/2016/02/icde08gsearch.pdf

98. T. Reza, Pattern Matching in Massive Metadata Graphs at Scale, 2019. https://doi.org/10.14288/1.0387453. Corpus ID: 212778128. https://open.library.ubc.ca/soa/cIRcle/collections/ubctheses/24/items/1.0387453

99. Pattern Recognition. https://en.wikipedia.org/wiki/Pattern_recognition

100. R. Van De Walker, Consciousness Is Pattern Recognition, 2016. https://arxiv.org/abs/1605.03009

101. Pattern Recognition (Psychology). https://en.wikipedia.org/wiki/Pattern_recognition_(psychology)

102. Pattern Language. https://en.wikipedia.org/wiki/Pattern_language
103. Pattern Language. https://en.wikipedia.org/wiki/Pattern_language#:~:
     text=A%20pattern%20language%20is%20an,1977%20book%20A%20
     Pattern%20Language
104. A Pattern Language. https://en.wikipedia.org/wiki/A_Pattern_Language
105. What Is a Pattern Language? https://groupworksdeck.org/pattern-
     language
106. C. Alexander, S. Ishikawa, M. Silverstein, et al., A Pattern Language:
     Towns, Buildings, Construction (Center for Environmental Structure
     Series). Oxford University Press, 1977. www.amazon.com/Pattern-
     Language-Buildings-Construction-Environmental/dp/0195019199
107. T. Winn, P. Calder, A Pattern Language for Pattern Language Structure.
     Appeared at Third Asian Pacific Conference on Pattern Languages of
     Programs (KoalaPLoP 2002), January 2003. www.researchgate.net/
     publication/228944468_A_pattern_language_for_pattern_language_
     structure
108. M. Hafiz, P. Adamczyk, R. Johnson, Growing a Pattern Language
     (for Security), Proceedings of the ACM International Symposium
     on New Ideas, New Paradigms, and Reflections on Programming
     and Software, October 2012. https://doi.org/10.1145/2384592.2384607.
     www.researchgate.net/publication/262211609_Growing_a_pattern_
     language_for_security
109. T. Iba, Pattern Languages as Media for the Creative Society, Journal
     of Information Processing and Management, 2013, 55(12). https://
     doi.org/10.1241/johokanri.55.865. www.researchgate.net/publication/
     255484746_Pattern_Languages_as_Media_for_the_Creative_Society
110. T. Iba, Change Making Patterns. A Pattern Language for Fostering Social
     Entrepreneurship. https://citeseerx.ist.psu.edu/viewdoc/download?
     doi=10.1.1.677.5339&rep=rep1&type=pdf
111. M. Van Welie, G. van der Veer, Pattern Languages in Interaction Design:
     Structure and Organization, October 2011. www.researchgate.net/
     publication/228881522_Pattern_languages_in_interaction_design_
     Structure_and_organization
112. G. Meszaros, J. Doble, A Pattern Language for Pattern Writing, The
     Hillside Group. https://hillside.net/index.php/a-pattern-language-for-
     pattern-writing
113. Integrity Awareness Initiative UN. Secretary-General. UN Secretariat,
     2005. https://digitallibrary.un.org/record/556931?ln=en
114. M. Mantell, What Is Conscious Integrity? https://mikemantell.com/
     conscious-integrity/
115. Are Consciousness and Awareness the Same? www.scienceandnonduality.
     com/article/are-consciousness-and-awareness-the-same
116. V. Hawks, A Pattern of Integrity. Agency, Order, and Obedience. https://
     rsc.byu.edu/moral-foundations-standing-firm-world-shifting-values/
     pattern-integrity
117. M. M. O'Hara, J. K. Wood, Patterns of Awareness: Consciousness and
     the Group Mind, Gestalt Journal, 1983, 6(2), 103–116. https://psycnet.
     apa.org/record/1984-25833-001

118. R. Van De Walker, Consciousness Is Pattern Recognition, 2016. https:// arxiv.org/abs/1605.03009

119. D. Filipenco, Top 10 World Problems and Their Solutions, 2 August 2022. www.developmentaid.org/news-stream/post/147458/top-10-world-problems-and-their-solutions

120. 100+ Ways to Heal the Planet. https://healtheplanet.com/100-ways-to-heal-the-planet/?gad=1&gclid=CjwKCAjwwb6lBhBJEiwAbu VUShK86HiW8uXefpY3xL4TuXJBh1JKb86k652trpLSUu OveyGoDyU0zRoCAxUQAvD_BwE

121. B. Wedge, Psychiatry and International Affairs, Science, 1967, 157(3786), 281–85. www.jstor.org/stable/1721793. Accessed 21 July 2023.

122. Why War? A Letter from Albert Einstein to Sigmund Freud. https://en.unesco.org/courier/may-1985/why-war-letter-albert-einstein-sigmund-freud

123. Why War? A Letter from Freud to Einstein. https://en.unesco.org/courier/marzo-1993/why-war-letter-freud-einstein